In memory of my wonderful mother, my little brother and all the other unforgettable members of my family who perished under degrading and squalid conditions in Nazi camps.

BOY 30529

A Memoir

FELIX WEINBERG

VERSO

London • New York

This paperback edition first published by Verso 2014
First published by Verso 2013
© Felix Weinberg 2013, 2014
Foreword © Suzanne Bardgett 2013, 2014

1 3 5 7 9 10 8 6 4 2

Verso

UK: 6 Meard Street, London W1F 0EG
US: 20 Jay Street, Suite 1010, Brooklyn, NY 11201
www.versobooks.com

Verso is the imprint of New Left Books

ISBN-13: 978-1-78168-300-2 (PBK)
eISBN-13: 978-1-78168-301-9 (US)
eISBN-13: 978-1-78168-479-5 (UK)

British Library Cataloguing in Publication Data
A catalogue record for this book is available from the British Library

The Library of Congress Has Cataloged the Hardback Edition as Follows

Weinberg, Felix Jiri, author.
Boy 30529 : a memoir / Felix Weinberg.
pages cm
ISBN 978-1-78168-078-0 (pbk. : alk. paper)
1. Weinberg, Felix Jiri – Childhood and youth.
2. Jews – Czech Republic – Prague – Biography.
3. Holocaust, Jewish (1939-1945)– Czech Republic –
Prague – Personal narratives. 4. Jewish children in
the Holocaust – Czech Republic – Prague –
Biography. 5. Auschwitz (Concentration camp)
6. Holocaust survivors – England – London –
Biography. 7. Prague (Czech Republic) –
Biography. I. Title.
DS135.C97W438 2012
940.53'18092– dc23
[B]
2012043156

Typeset in Fournier MT by Hewer Text UK Ltd, Edinburgh
Printed by in the US by Maple Vail

BOY 30529

Contents

Foreword by Suzanne Bardgett   ix

Acknowledgements   xiii

Preface   xvii

PART I: CHILDHOOD

Chapter 1: The Golden Years   1

Chapter 2: Dark Clouds   19

Chapter 3: The End of Hope   35

PART II: THE CAMPS

Chapter 4: Holocaust Literature and Reality   53

Chapter 5: Ghetto Theresienstadt (Terezín)   57

Chapter 6: Auschwitz-Birkenau   67

Contents

Chapter 7: Blechhammer   81

Chapter 8: The Longest Walk, The Coldest Train Journey   99

Chapter 9: Buchenwald   109

PART III: THE RETURN

Chapter 10: Prague   129

Chapter 11: Ústí nad Orlicí   133

PART IV: ENGLAND

Chapter 12: A Lancaster Bomber   145

Chapter 13: My Father   151

Chapter 14: Natural Philosophy   157

Appendix: Chronology 1942–45   167

Foreword

Back in the mid 1990s, our small team of researchers at the Imperial War Museum were accumulating what they could for the Holocaust Exhibition then being planned for Millennium Year. It was a busy and rather anxious time. We were trying – with some difficulty – to amass a collection of artefacts for the showcases, and each time a researcher came back from a visit to a survivor with a relic of the concentration camps, it seemed that a further piece of our exhibition was in place.

I remember a particularly unusual item – a battered leather jacket – arriving in the project office. Its donor, Professor Felix Weinberg, described it as 'on permanent, if unauthorised, loan from one of the defunct Buchenwald guards'.

The 'liberated' SS jacket duly went into the Holocaust exhibition, and in due course I met Felix Weinberg and his wife, Jill. I realised that our donor, who had grown up in Czechoslovakia, was an eminent professor of physics at Imperial College London and briefly wondered how he had managed to make that long journey – from child survivor of a series of concentration camps to esteemed professor of science. Professor Weinberg mentioned to me that he had worn the SS guard's jacket for many years when riding his motorbike in London, and I remember thinking this showed an admirably defiant attitude to his past captivity.

Several years later – in 2011 – Felix Weinberg got in touch again. He had decided that he owed it to his family to write an account of his early life, and wondered whether I would like to read it. I did so and was struck by several things: firstly, Felix has extraordinary powers of recollection – being able to transport the reader into his teenage mind, where a spirit of scientific enquiry was already taking root. This ability to resurrect his boyhood enthusiasm for how things work, overlaid with the wisdom of later years, and considerable self-awareness, makes it an especially engaging and original read.

Secondly, it is clear just how much Felix Weinberg's eventual survival of Terezín, Auschwitz-Birkenau, Blechhammer, Gross-Rosen and Buchenwald camps owes to the 'cocooning' of his early years. A father who loved playing with his two boys and a mother with an instinctive ability to bring fun into her children's lives – these were the wellspring from which Felix would draw during his two-and-a-half-year captivity. To dream of his past life – enriched by doting grandparents, journeys by paddle-steamer on the Elbe and trips by horse-drawn sleigh – only to wake up in the stench and misery of the concentration camp barracks was excruciating. But it was these memories – together with the chance inner reserves that came from having a father who was a fitness and nutrition fanatic – which enabled the young Felix to survive.

Hunger, ill treatment and finally the trauma of Allied bombing left Felix 'half-alive' at the end of the war. His closing chapters lay bare aspects of the liberation of the camps I had not heard about – the 'Wild-West interregnum' before the arrival of proper relief organisations saw child survivors blowing themselves up with weapons taken from the arsenal abandoned by the Nazis. The almost apocalyptic scenes Felix witnessed at this point, and their tragic aftermath, stayed with him forever.

To revisit the past in this way cannot have been easy. All those who care about the proper documenting of this horrendous era must be grateful to Felix Weinberg for giving us this insightful and ultimately uplifting account.

Suzanne Bardgett, Head of Research
Imperial War Museum
September 2011

Acknowledgements

This chronicle would never have seen the light of day but for the influence of a number of good friends. First and foremost it was Bea Green – herself a 'Kindertransportee', who arrived in the UK before the war and is something of an activist in keeping the memory of those events alive – who insisted that I owed it to my children and grandchildren to record this history, no matter how harrowing, because they 'had the right to know'. Next, a number of friends and colleagues who asked to see what I had written urged me to share it with a wider readership because, to my utter astonishment, they thought it a 'good read'. Amongst them I am indebted to Drs James Lawton, Darren Tymens, Ivan Vince, professors Charmian Brinson, Rafael and Deniz Kandiyoti and, in particular, three other camp survivors with rather different histories: Peter Frank, Otto Jakubovic, and his wife Angela, as well as Frank Bright. Some of my friends were also most helpful in drawing my attention to omissions and slip-ups, and I can only hope, considering how ancient some of us have become, that I have now succeeded in rectifying most of them.

I am deeply grateful to Suzanne Bardgett not only for writing such a moving foreword but also for providing the one and only opportunity for the 'Czech boys' of my narrative and their descendants and families to meet (some thirty-five in all) at the Imperial War Museum in September 2005. Suzanne arranged the screening of a film of the children climbing into bombers for the flight to England in the autumn of 1945, arranged afternoon tea, and gave us the opportunity to see her magnificent work in keeping the memories of our World War II experiences in public view.

Regarding the battered leather jacket which she mentions and which now graces her display: if there were a prize for the world's ugliest garment, I would back it as a leading contender. I do not think it was ever designed to be worn on the outside; my guess is it was originally intended to be worn under the Luftwaffe uniform by flight crews operating at high altitudes in order to keep them warm. The main body was stitched together from a large number of small squares of fleece, with the sickly off-white-wash leather facing outward. The sleeves were knitted and loosely attached at the shoulders. The design spoke of a nation poor in material resources but well endowed with slave labour. What made it such a valuable prize, first for a Buchenwald guard and then for me – to the point that I brought it on the Lancaster Bomber for the flight to England – was that it was uncommonly warm, and certainly the warmest undergarment I ever owned. Perhaps I ought to mention that the Buchenwald guard raised no objections to my taking it, as he was dead at the time, possibly due to an earlier visit by some of my fellow prisoners.

Acknowledgements

Before exposing the jacket to public view on my motorcycle, I made a questionable improvement to its dead sheep exterior appearance by dyeing the leather, using a deep-brown suede shoe dye. That is how it appears today. My children remember me washing the car in it – perhaps because of the embarrassment it caused them. I am sure that, at the time of presenting it to the IWM, nothing was further from my mind than writing up my wartime experiences. Still, it was the first time it came to me that some apparently totally useless things might be worth preserving for posterity rather than ending up in a ragbag, so perhaps a seed had been sown.

Felix Weinberg
16 September 2011

Preface

A difficult decision

The Fellows' Room at the Royal Society looks out on the Mall and the rows of beautiful trees lining the edge of St James's Park between Buckingham Palace and Admiralty Arch. I have again misjudged public transport and arrived far too early for a meeting, so I decide I might as well sit in a room with a view, plush chairs, coffee, and internet access. I keep meaning to work here more often. On this occasion I have, unusually, some spare time to think and I have a most difficult decision to make. Having tried for the last sixty-five years to forget and erase from my memory my teenage experiences in Auschwitz and other Nazi concentration camps, I am now being persuaded that I owe it to my family and others to write them up.

The subject was hardly ever mentioned within the family. That was due largely to Jill, my beloved wife, who devotedly looked after me and our three sons, until she died in January 2006, two years after our Golden Wedding Anniversary. She had probably herself been traumatised by my behaviour during nightmares in the early days and clearly resolved to protect the children from dwelling on the subject. The story that daddy had such a bad memory that he had to have his telephone number tattooed on his forearm had a short lifetime but it set a pattern. I would, in fact, not have minded talking about what happened but found it convenient to go along with this state of affairs, for a different reason: I did not want to define myself as being 'a camp survivor'.

I am left wondering if I can find the time, in view of all my other commitments, for what must be a most painful and harrowing undertaking for me. Yet it does seem right that my children should learn more about the wonderful grandmother and other close family members they never knew. I am eighty-two years old. If I do not start now, it will not be done.

It occurs to me that this building is haunted by some of the ghosts that prey on my mind and are looking over my shoulder as I try to decide. Until 1938 at least part of this great edifice was the German Embassy. I have an uneasy feeling that I may well be sitting in the very same place where, seventy years earlier, Joachim von Ribbentrop, Hitler's Foreign Minister and Ambassador to Britain, took part in hatching the plans that would destroy millions of lives, including those of my nearest and dearest.

On 16 October 1946, Ribbentrop was the first Nazi politician to be hanged following the Nuremberg trials. That was to be expected; it seemed right and just to me. What was absolutely not to be expected was that I had survived and was already in England at the time. That happened by way of a succession of near miracles, which I have set down in the following pages.

PART I

Childhood

I

The Golden Years

There is an early photograph in my possession of my parents' wedding – Victor Weinberg, twenty-nine, bachelor of Aussig, to Nelly Maria Altschul, twenty-four, spinster of Prague. The date is chalked on the synagogue door in ornate script. I was born on 2 April 1928, exactly nine months after that date, as befitted our well-regulated family life. They named me Felix Georg, yet no one ever called me George. When I arrived in England, seventeen years later, I had rejected all things German and gave my middle name as Jiří, the Czech for George. There was no going back after I had published some papers and books under the initials F. J.

That is how it came about that I now have a middle name that my nearest and dearest are quite unable to pronounce.

I had a very happy childhood. It came to an end too soon and too abruptly, thanks to Adolf Hitler, but I believe it is the early years that count. They furnish the mind with a cocoon of security and contentment into which it can withdraw in times of hardship. That is why the children of dysfunctional families never stand a chance, in my view. My cocoon was well equipped with cosy memories and certainties of having been much loved and cherished.

My recollections of childhood are very much affected by having had to move frequently from one home to another. During the first years of my life, my father, an industrial chemist, had a factory of his own in a small place near Aussig (Ústí nad Labem in Czech) called Türmitz (Trmice). What little I know about it is influenced by impressions largely gleaned from looking at old photographs. Most prominently, there were two large Alsatian guard dogs. In fact, my first memory is of two large slobbering dogs' muzzles, overflowing with very large teeth, peering into my pram. Just a single flashback; I suppose that the expectation of imminently being about to be eaten would leave a lasting impression at a very early age.

I also remember my nanny in a sort of nurse's outfit pushing me in my pram. A quite likely alternative is that, knowing what my pram and she actually looked like from photographs, my mind manufactured the memory. My first coherent recollections, however, date from the time after we had moved into my 'proper home', a large house which overlooked the big cobbled market square in the centre of Aussig. The house was owned by my grandfather, I believe, who lived in a flat above ours with his divorced daughter, Else, my father's older sister. We were on the third floor. There was a lift and there were the rails left over from what must have been a little railway through the arch on the ground floor of the house, which led to the yard and the office of my grandfather who had a business in agricultural produce.

Every Saturday was market day and the whole square was covered in stalls with umbrellas. Every Saturday also my grandfather went to the market and bought a pigeon for my dinner.

I remember the layout of our flat as a long corridor with rooms leading off it. The bedrooms were at the back end, with a balcony overlooking the yard where my grandfather had his office. Beyond that yard was a beer garden under spreading chestnut trees. During summer nights, when we slept with windows open, the loud output of an oompah band from the inn was my nightly lullaby. At the other end of the corridor were two adjacent elegant rooms overlooking the square. A grand piano stood in one, and I was allowed to practise on it, usually with my mother. The other was full of paintings, fragile china and other *objets d'art* and was out of bounds, except when used for entertaining guests or on festive occasions.

At right angles to the long corridor were other rooms accessed from a central lounge. On one side was a room where my mother did her etching. That also contained a large wind-up gramophone, just like the HMV trademark, minus the dog. On the opposite side there was the kitchen and pantry – the domain of Marie, our cook. Marie had two handicaps: a huge goitre and the fact she was an unmarried mother. Of these, the latter was the greater affliction. That part of Bohemia must have been an iodine-deficient area, as goitres were not that uncommon. Iodised salt came in much later. Having a child out of wedlock, on the other hand, was a terrible stigma in those days, and Marie was eternally grateful to my father for employing her full-time and allowing her time off to be with little Rolli (a diminutive for Roland) on Sundays and, occasionally, to bring him to our home. I suspect that she would not have been able to keep him otherwise.

The view from the kitchen window was to the centre of the flats, not accessible from our floor. There was a glass-covered top of an old lift shaft, which terrified me because of the story of a maid falling to her death through the glass. The most exciting event that happened in that kitchen occurred when my mother started a fire, which actually required the attention of the fire brigade. She was melting wax for her etching. It overheated and caught fire. My mother, who evidently had very little scientific background, then tried to put it out by pouring water over the burning pan, which converted it into a flame-thrower and caused the conflagration to spread to the rest of the kitchen. The arrival of the firemen in their theatrical helmets clearly made a lasting impression on me.

Several memories centre on my bedroom: the earliest is of biting my mother's nose hard enough to make it bleed. That beautiful, loveable nose was right in front of my face as she was dressing me, so I took a bite, out of pure affection. I am afraid I got a slap, though it was chiefly self-defence and shock on her part. I could not have explained that it was pure love on mine.

A more serious incident involved my bedside lamp, which

My mother and her loveable nose

had a metal lampshade with a very sharp edge. We had just come back from holiday and I was very tired. There was a heavy thunderstorm that night and I had a nightmare. I dreamed about something that led up to an explosion involving a bright flash of light and a loud bang. I leapt up, still hearing the roll of thunder, and cut my eyelid on the sharp lampshade; I carry the scar to this day. I remember my parents rushing in, and how horrified my mother was to see me with blood streaming from my eye down my cheek, thinking that I had lost an eye. It proved to me that dreams happen instantaneously, since it took only the moment of the lightning flash and thunder for my brain to make up the whole story of my nightmare.

During the holidays we used to visit my mother's parents in Prague. These were major expeditions, as I recollect, with all the staff involved in packing trunks at least a week in advance. We stayed for a week or a fortnight during Christmas holidays, except for my father who had to return to work. A taxi took us to the station, which was, in fact, only a short walk away. Distances in general seem to have shrunk since those days; I was totally amazed when I revisited, after the war, to discover that Prague could scarcely be more than seventy miles from Aussig and we did the journey by bus in about two hours. Perhaps one needs to scale dimensions according to one's height.

Prague itself was my first big city and is, in my opinion, still the most beautiful in central Europe. My grandparents' flat was in a large house (an embassy, last time I looked) facing a park, just round the corner from the main square (Wenceslas). I had never before see neon advertisements that moved! I remember a multicoloured one of a grenadier firing a cannon, the shell from which exploded after a trajectory so long it extended the length of the square, the blast revealing a tin of a well-known boot polish. There was a famous fish restaurant (Ryba – it was still there after the war) with a big shop window that was a giant aquarium.

These visits to my grandparents were pure magic. Their flat was palatial and ornate, full of paintings, valuable art objects and Victorian knick-knacks. My grandmother was very beautiful and bedecked with jewellery. My grandfather had enough

On the balcony of my grandparents' flat with my brother, pretending to read a
borrowed newspaper through borrowed glasses.

leisure and money to indulge in a great variety of hobbies. He
built radios at a time when that was quite unusual. He had a
movie camera and a projector and gave performances of early
movies and cartoons such as *Felix the Cat*. In winter we had
snowball fights in the park just outside the front door. The flat
boasted what must have been one of the earliest refrigerators,
operated by a small gas flame. In the toilet there was an electric
fire, which came on automatically when the light was turned on.
It was an enchanted castle to me.

When I was three and a bit, I ceased to be the centre of attention in the household because my little brother was born. My
father with his Germanic background must have been responsible for my brother being named Hans Gerhard, straight out of
the *Nibelungen*. The strict translation of Hans is Hanuš (which is

With my grandparents in the garden of their summer retreat in a suburb of Prague

how his name now appears in archival documents) but he was called Jan in Czech and we called him Jeníček, which is the diminutive. He was a dear little baby and there were other compensations for my being dethroned. The family policy was to have a Christmas tree with presents underneath every December for the first four years of a child's life before changing over to Chanukah (that was about the limit of our religious observance). My brother brought me a three-year extension of Christmases.

I believe that he had a new nurse and about the same time I acquired a *Fräulein* – or rather a *Slečna* – a very charming young Czech lady with a brand new teacher's diploma. (*Slečna* = 'miss', but somehow neither 'nanny', 'governess' nor 'au pair' quite fits the bill.) I am not sure she even spoke German. I suspect that the idea was to make me speak Czech most of the time, in preparation for school. We were bilingual (my parents also spoke French and English; my knowledge of English was confined to one phrase: 'Not in front of the children!', generally said rather loudly and associated with parental arguments). In 1932, when the citizens of the Sudeten had to choose, my parents opted for Czech nationality though my father's Czech was never perfect.

I ought perhaps to stress that under Masaryk, the first President and founder of Czechoslovakia – an enlightened statesman, sociologist and philosopher – the country was a true democracy. He died when I was seven and was replaced by Beneš, a lesser but equally decent man. I regard it as a great tragedy that this benevolent regime existed for just twenty years. Yet I was fortunate in that my childhood coincided with the second half of that enlightened period, which was written out of history by the Cold War Communist regime.

Aussig was quite a large town, perhaps the third largest in Bohemia, with 44,000 inhabitants in those days. Although it was industrialised, it was surrounded by the most beautiful countryside. The River Elbe, bordered by vineyards (*weinbergs*!) and ruins of castles on crags, dominate the memories of my idyllic childhood. It's where I learned to swim and where we spent summer weekends cruising in paddle steamers to a succession of small resorts. Each of them had an inn by a landing stage and each café specialised in some particular kind of dessert. Our family, friends and relatives would settle down to coffee and the local speciality cakes, while my father went for a long walk and, when I got a little older, he dragged me along.

Talking of being dragged along reminds me of a painful episode when I got caught on a fishing line by one of the many anglers along the river. I saw the fishing line snaking through the grass, so I picked it up in blissful ignorance of the walking angler dragging it behind him at one end and the hook at the other. The inevitable consequence was that the angler found that he had hooked, by his finger, a loudly yelling little boy who was running behind him as fast as his short

Big brother, little brother on holiday

fat legs would carry him. I remember the episode mainly because my mother found the scene so irresistibly funny that, instead of rushing to my rescue, she was convulsed with laughter, whereupon I called her a 'silly cow' – which was not met with the sympathetic understanding the circumstances merited, in my view.

In winter we went skiing. I had my first short skis at the age of four. The nearest makeshift ski slopes were only as far as the terminus of the tram that passed our house, at a place called Telnitz. At weekends we were allowed to put our skis on the tram and I believe that it was only about half an hour's ride from our home. Sometimes we went for cross-country expeditions further afield, staying overnight in ski chalets in the mountains. I loved the forests covered in deep snow. The only problem was that my father was an excellent and totally fearless skier, neither of which attributes could truthfully be applied to the rest of the family. His expectation that we would keep up with him used to cause me some anxiety.

At Eastertime we went to a ski hut/hotel at the Keilberg. That involved a train journey followed by a long ride in a horse-drawn sleigh. The luggage went into the back and I was allowed to sit next to the driver with a blanket across my knees. The horse was also covered by a blanket and suffered from flatulence. I was greatly intrigued by its passing wind, not least because it could be perceived by three senses; apart from the two obvious ones, the farts were also visible as little clouds of steam.

With *Slečna* at the Keilberg ski resort

Whenever going on holiday involved an early morning start, my mother used to wake us children with a special song she composed for the purpose, just to enhance our sense of excitement. It worked so well that, although my excitement caused me to wake much earlier, I pretended to be asleep in anticipation of her creeping through the door.

My mother was very talented. As a young girl, she had been sent to finishing schools in England and Switzerland, spoke five languages, and spent her spare time playing the piano (and teaching me to play – both the piano and the harmonica) and producing beautiful etchings on glass and metal objects. I believe that she rebelled against her privileged and affluent upbringing by developing strongly socialist leanings. That affected me mainly in the books she gave me to read. She was active in WIZO (Women's International Zionist Organisation), which had the left-wing policies of the early kibbutzim at its heart. The greatest benefit to me when I was little was the pure joy of participating in her tea parties for lots of Jewish ladies and, in particular, the shopping expeditions beforehand. The shopkeepers always offered samples to taste and my expert opinion on various salamis, cheeses, etcetera was clearly in great demand. (I am still addicted to salamis, anchovy pâté and other constituents of my mother's nibbles.) The only downside was having to play with the children of my mother's acquaintances. To the best of my recollection, none of them had sons; all I can remember is having to be polite to lots of really obnoxious little girls who wanted to play their games, their way. I much preferred being included in my mother's excursions with her friends to exclusive gourmet coffee houses. I didn't share in coffee and gossip but I did in tasting the cakes; marzipan 'potatoes' in particular left a lasting impression

Clearly, my mother did not live by my father's dictum (one of many) that one should stop eating when food tastes the best. If my father taught me iron self-discipline, I learned from my mother that applying that to cutting out treats would be overdoing things – a point of view that I was, and am still, all too ready to adopt. She did diet, intermittently. What mattered to the family was that she was wonderfully imaginative and loved us deeply – a love she often expressed by writing us poems and children's books which she illustrated with beautiful watercolours.

My father's provincial upbringing and background did not match my mother's Prague–patrician milieu. He, on the other hand, was the first graduate in the family and established our family's academic leaning. Indeed he was forever arranging additional classes for me. One outlandish bee in his bonnet concerned my having to learn to write German Gothic script. So I had a teacher who came in the evenings to teach me. I still cannot get my head around that. It might have turned out to be useful had the Third Reich indeed lasted a thousand years – as Hitler so spectacularly overestimated – but hardly to a nice Jewish boy!

To understand my father better, it is necessary to know something about his early years. His mother died when he was a child. He had an older brother who, in due course, inherited his father's business and ruined it, and an older sister, Else, of whom more later. So, when he turned seventeen, his father bought him a horse (called Betty) and he volunteered to join the Austro-Hungarian mounted artillery. Czechoslovakia, of course, did not exist before the Great War, but was part of the Austro-Hungarian Empire. My father liked to talk about his military exploits and kept his service revolver, a medal and a piece of shrapnel extracted from his buttock hidden in a green shoebox in the top drawer of the wardrobe. That piece of shrapnel prevented him from completing his chemistry degree since, at the crucial time, he could not stand for his practical exams. He made a complete recovery, however, and appeared to be quite proud of the additional aperture in his bottom. The lack of a degree did not seem to affect his career as a chemist or his activism as a health fanatic.

I probably shouldn't cavil at being force-fed all those vitamins and minerals which may have helped me to survive the next war, but I am still under the influence of some of his dicta to this day. I suspect the fact I have stumpy teeth may not be unrelated to being instructed to chew each mouthful thirty-two times. Dabbling in food chemistry convinced my father that something distasteful could be made more palatable by adding some attractive flavour, no matter how incompatible. The memory of his emulsions of cod liver oil with raspberry juice still makes me shudder. He was also very keen on me doing physical exercises. We had rings, interchangeable with a horizontal bar, hanging from the nursery door lintel. For a period I acquired a personal trainer to do press-ups and other calisthenics with me. He was a giant of a man, very affable, and we soon worked out that what we, both of us, liked to do best was for him to gallop around the flat, carrying me on his shoulders. When my father discovered this, it was the (unlamented) end of my career as a gymnast.

If I did not get closer to my father in my childhood, it was mainly because he was never there during the week. His work involved him travelling far and wide with samples of chemicals. When he returned late on Friday nights and my mother got tired of waiting for him in bed, she generally found him asleep in the bath with the newspaper floating on the, by then stone-cold, water. Yet he influenced my life in many ways for which I shall always be thankful. Aside from all the minerals, vitamins and, yes, even the kohlrabi and grated raw carrots with lemon juice, which probably helped me survive the camps, there were the outings. Every weekend and often during holidays we travelled to beautiful nature spots. He taught me to love nature. I had stacks of books on birds, plants, trees and every creepy-crawly under the sun, together with equipment for collecting and studying them. My father was, and remained to the end of his life, a decent, upright, principled man.

And so to primary school, at the age of six. The bad news was that I had lost my lovely *Slečna*. The good news was that, to my utter amazement, she turned up as my class teacher. I had to stand when she entered the classroom – that was a weird turn of events. There was a, to me, painful gulf between us now, but she was an excellent teacher. In domestic science she taught us – boys as well as girls – how to sew on buttons and darn socks among other useful skills. In that way she also contributed to my survival in Buchenwald ten years later. The fact that I excelled in most subjects complicated the issue of not being regarded as teacher's pet (though I doubt that any of the other pupils were aware of our previous association). Fortunately I managed to be bottom of the class in singing (accused of 'growling') and, more particularly, in handwriting. We used penholders with steel nibs, which we dipped into inkwells that were periodically refilled by the school janitor. Those naughty boys were forever experimenting with the revolting smells that could be produced by stuffing food residues into inkwells and leaving them to decay there. The consequent lumps in the ink were the cause of my downfall – that's my excuse, anyway, for covering my work in more spectacular inkblots than anyone else ever managed to achieve.

I could attend my primary school for three years only and I have the happiest memories of it. I cried in my first days there when I was told that it was closed at weekends. It was a short walk just round the corner from our house. In winter I would walk through streets covered in thick snow and I remember with nostalgia the warm classroom with its hissing gas lamps providing cosy yellow illumination.

Now there is a big car park where my school used to be. The school was next door to a beautiful monastery, which, under the Communist regime, was used as a furniture store. I believe that the Communists did more to destroy the beauty of my home-town than the Germans ever did. They had more time, after all. They did away with our lovely cobbled square and built ugly buildings all over it.

2

Dark Clouds

We had, in the Sudeten, our own home-grown mini-Hitler in the form of Konrad Henlein, leader of the SDP (Sudetendeutsche Partei). Our rooms overlooking the central square had a grandstand view of his podium and the brown-shirt rallies from my earliest days. Although they did not have swastikas, they had flags and red armbands bearing a white disk as background to some black insignia not unlike a swastika, and they marched up and down the streets shouting aggressive slogans, which made us feel very threatened. I do not know whether that was a factor in our moving house again; in retrospect it does not seem like a propitious time for my parents to have bought a new villa. Although Henlein exuded menace, I believe even then I sensed something gruesomely ludicrous in their goose-stepping in jackboots, not to mention his appeal to Hitler that he needed protection from the Czechs for his band of thugs.

What I found quite hilarious, many years later, relates to Henlein's problems with his origins, in view of his outspoken policy against mixed marriages – which in this instance concerned the Slav Untermensch, never mind Jews. To his discomfiture, his mother's father was Czech. He solved the problem by changing his still-living mother's name from Dvořáček to Dworatschek, which may look more German but is as near as one can get to the Czech in pronunciation. Grotesquely, that was sufficient to support his career, in due course, as a high Nazi official.

But I am running far ahead of my narrative. We probably had to move anyway because my first school offered only two years of primary education and I suppose I needed to be within walking distance of a larger school. My parents bought a beautiful new villa in Kleische (Klíše), which was in the suburbs of Aussig, a long way from my childhood home by the picturesque main square in the centre. It was called Villa Rose, in Luizina Street. So the move to the new villa was the third complete transformation of my life by the age of ten.

My parents must have been involved in designing features of the house, if not the house itself. There was a veranda topped by a terrace on which my father had showers installed. I think his idea was that we would do our exercises in the fresh air and then have a healthy, presumably cold, shower. In the middle of the garden was a weeping willow, which enfolded a summerhouse, in the middle of which was a round table surrounded by a circular bench. The tree trunk grew through a hole in the centre of the table. It took me a little while to work out that the table must have been built around the tree, as it would have been difficult to direct the tree to grow through the hole. The effect was very pleasing because the branches hung all the way to the ground so that, when the weeping willow was in leaf, one could not actually see the summerhouse and had to part the branches to reveal it and to find its entrance.

I saw the exterior of the villa again half a century later, after the war and the demise of the Iron Curtain, on a brief visit with my wife and it had hardly changed. Someone had added a garage and the latest owner did not open the door when we rang the bell. I would have loved just to look inside, but perhaps they were out, or perhaps they were suspicious of strange characters standing outside comparing their house with an ancient photograph.

In spite of the beautiful house, its surroundings, and the proximity of my favourite swimming pool, our move to Klíše was the beginning of a very unhappy time. First, my maternal grandparents died. My grandfather had had a stroke a year or so earlier, which completely paralysed him. He was in a wheelchair and could communicate only by blinking. I was told that all he ever asked for was that, if only someone would wheel him to the lift door, he thought he would find the strength to throw himself down the lift shaft.

Next, my grandmother had to go into hospital. I think she must have had a hysterectomy or something similar, not to be detailed in front of the children. The day she was due to return home, while my mother was looking forward to travelling to Prague to collect her, she had a pulmonary embolism which proved fatal.

So I lost my beloved grandparents and my sole reason to visit Prague. At the same time, my little brother developed a nervous complaint of some kind. He spoke of pains all over his body. He had a phobia about electrical equipment giving him shocks. I think he must have had a real electric shock at some stage and that precipitated some anxiety condition in his mind. That may not have been unconnected to the threat of war, which started a lot earlier in the Sudeten, because we were in the front line of the Hitler menace. I still have a bad conscience, because, at the age of nine and ten, all the preparation for war excited me and I told my brother things that may well have aggravated his fears. His panic attacks were intermittent and unpredictable and his screaming in terror horrified me. I have always been overwhelmed by pity for people who act irrationally; I have often had to be stopped from approaching drunks in the street.

On top of all that, I hated and feared my new school. Our class teacher was a young man who had just come out of the army and was some kind of sadist. Every school day started with the ceremony of his beating the children who had not handed in their homework or were guilty of some other made-up misdemeanour. He called out a list of names, had them bend over a desk and beat them in front of the class with something like a slipper. It actually never happened to me – I continued to do very well – but I was terrified that it might. Previously I had always loved going to school; this was the first time I understood why most children do not.

The other aspect I did not like about that school was that there were children from really poor homes, who were actually hungry. I had not known about not having enough to eat. I suppose that the school must have been established in what used to be an underprivileged area, until recently built luxury villas brought in an influx of professional Czech parents. My mother always used to provide me with elevenses, as did others of our background, and poor children used to beg for a bit of bread or a piece of my apple, which I found quite harrowing. I do not think I ever learned anything there, or made any friends.

I developed an interesting defence mechanism when things got on top of me at school: abdominal pains, which required me to be excused to go home at once. That may not have been unconnected to stress, not to mention a diet rich in the detested kohlrabi. I could hardly have been described as a sickly child, but my winter colds generally led to bronchitis. The reason, I now believe, is that I had a radical tonsillectomy at the age of four.

I should have mentioned that operation earlier, when I listed my earliest memories, because I clearly recall the feeling of suffocation associated with ether anaesthesia, when what looked like a large shower head was clamped over my face. In those days my parents favoured surgical removal for any body parts that might cause problems in later life; I was lucky to escape with my appendix and teeth intact. The hospital was in Prague and my mother shared the ward with me. The German word for tonsils is synonymous with 'almonds'. I do not know what my mother imagined they would look like but she asked to keep them as souvenirs. When they were brought to her, pickled in formalin, my mother passed out, so I have never seen my tonsils. But I digress.

I loved being a bit ill because I had such a lovely time in bed. Out came all my stacks of children's comics and favourite books. Sometimes prolonging this happy state needed a little help. In those days the two standard methods of 'ridding the body of toxins' were enemas for anything below the belt and sweating it out for ailments higher up. The latter was achieved with the aid of an aspirin plus hot tea and lots of blankets. As the standard diagnostic was temperature taken under the armpit with a clinical thermometer for ten, generally unsupervised, minutes, the availability of hot tea provided an easy method of preventing my temperature from reverting to its healthy 36.6°C too early. The tea was far hotter, of course, so the skill lay in shaking the mercury down, after a quick immersion, to what would constitute a credible rate of recovery from my illness. Unfortunately, I blew it irreversibly when, on one occasion, the tea was so hot, or the immersion time so long, that I was unable to see the top of the mercury. My mother, after some initial trauma, refused to believe I was at death's door and thereafter supervised the thermometry.

The next major upheaval in my life, in the fateful summer of 1938, coincided with what was to be the most exciting holiday ever, not least because it was to be abroad and I was to see the sea for the first time. Our previous holidays were always spent in the mountains and the countryside. The way it went was that my father would go ahead and book some picturesque farmhouse somewhere in the mountains and we would move in for the summer. My father would go back to work and visit only occasionally, perhaps at weekends, or for a week's break. He always arranged everything in advance; my mother never had to lift a finger. That, incidentally, may well have been a factor in the ultimate tragedy that destroyed our family.

Belgium was the destination of our first foreign holiday as a family. My parents had tried to go abroad without us just once before (it may have been to Dubrovnik). We were sent to a bracing children's holiday camp, and I think I was supposed to

Little brother getting a lift from father during a stiff climb in the Šumava mountains.

keep an eye on my brother; something I was never very good at, I am afraid.

It turned into a disaster. All the children took lunch at long trestle tables out in the open. This was at some distance from our dormitories, out on a steep meadow, set in beautiful mountain scenery. My brother always had been a slow eater and was being shouted at by the other children, who were keen to get going on whatever outing was planned for that afternoon. He executed a spectacular somersault when running downhill towards us and fell heavily. When he did not stop crying all that afternoon and all night, our caretakers eventually decided that perhaps he wasn't just making a fuss. Poor little Jeníček was loaded onto a small wooden cart and bumped over rutted country roads, screaming with pain all the way, to the nearest hospital, where a broken collarbone was diagnosed and set in plaster.

Our parents returned on overnight trains. My father, who had suffered a broken collarbone during the war, immediately decided that the plaster was wrongly positioned. After our return to Aussig, following an X-ray, the bone had to be re-broken and reset. The only positive outcome of this sad episode was that our parents never again went on holiday without us.

So this time we were all to go abroad and I was going to see the sea. In the days before long-distance air travel, Czech children generally never saw, and could barely imagine, an expanse of water so big that one could not see the other side. My mother, who was brilliant at working up a state of happy excitement in us children, kept preparing me for the enormous impression of first clapping eyes on such an incredible sight. It was also to be our longest journey ever by train, and we would even sleep on board. It did, of course, involve crossing Germany. I can only suppose it was planned so long in advance that the political situation at the time of departure could not have been foreseen. I would like to think that the possible opportunity of not coming back had crossed my parents' mind but subsequent actions showed no sign of such foresight.

By that time Germany was already in upheaval and, although I was not really aware of the political problems, or of any danger posed by Nazi anti-Semitism, it was obvious the trains were full of German soldiers, this being the summer prior to Hitler's invasion of the Sudeten. It was clear also that my parents were anxious to maintain a low profile. Overnight, they gave up their seats and stood in the corridor to allow us children to sleep stretched out on the train benches. The circumstance that we all looked considerably more Aryan than Hitler or any of his gang was an obvious asset. My little brother in particular, with his straw-blond hair and blue eyes looked the epitome of a Hitler Youth and tended to benefit from much unsolicited head-patting.

What has always puzzled me about the Nazi idealisation of Nordic looks and race is the appearance of their own pantheon of leaders. It is not just Hitler's swarthy Chaplinesque appearance and gestures; it is the whole Nazi leader Valhalla – the five-foot-four club-footed Goebbels, the jelly-bellied Reichs-marschall Goering. However did they get away with portraying themselves as exemplars of Aryan perfection without being laughed off the stage? Hitler survived assassination attempts, but being laughed at would have done for him politically and would have saved Europe from catastrophe. It has been said that Germans have no sense of humour but I have seen them roaring with laughter at people falling over. Why was this not in the same category? (I learned much later that the pebble-glassed Heinrich Himmler, the extermination camps' supremo, was in charge of racial purity issues as a result of his earlier obsession with breeding white chickens during his unsuccessful attempt to make a living as a poultry farmer. The most inventive of satirists could not have come up with that one. It would be hilarious were it not for the millions of lives lost.)

The place my father booked in Belgium was part farm, part pension, behind sand dunes in a small resort called Wenduine, somewhere between Oostende and Blankenberge. I believe the reason for his choice was chiefly its renowned cuisine. The ladies there came from a family who used to cook for the Empress Maria Theresa and we were the only guests at the time. I will try not to dwell on food again but that was the first time in my life I tasted West European white bread; I had never even seen shrimps or prawns before. My stomach has always had a long memory and the delicacies I encountered in Belgium, such as tomatoes stuffed with crevettes and homemade mayonnaise or crevette vol-au-vents, became something I tried particularly hard to avoid remembering during the subsequent hungry war years.

The house we stayed at was on the seaward edge of marshy farmland and cattle pasture. Then there was the coastal road, extensive dunes and the beach. Between the dunes and the beach ran a little yellow tram, all the way between Oostende and Blankenberge, stopping at all the small villages in between. It might be difficult to convey to a London commuter how much pleasure may be derived from public transport. The tramline wound around the dunes, providing occasional vistas of the sea, and our fellow passengers often included live chickens on the way to market.

My first sight of the sea actually happened at Blankenberge, quite a sizeable seaside resort and port. Each of the streets ending in a T-junction at the beach promenade had a big hump in it much higher than I was tall. My mother made us close our eyes just before the hump and open them on its apex so we took in the view all at once. And there was the sea: vast, endless, stretching to the horizon, merging with it in some weathers. The first impression was like a hammer blow. The masts of ships approaching over the horizon were indeed visible long before the rest hove into view, so the improbable story of the world being round was not just something you learned at school.

Belgium was the best holiday of my life. I swam in the sea, I learned to ride a bicycle on the promenade at Oostende, I went on a sea-going boat for the first time ever (I was left in charge of my brother, as my mother was so seasick that she locked herself in the toilet for most of the journey, deaf to the frantic hammering on the door). I learned to fly a kite and got a box kite of my own. It was a wonderful, unforgettable time all round.

Several memories stick in my mind. One was that there were terrifying thunderstorms at night – almost every night. The other was that we were plagued by mosquitoes. Every evening my brother and I were rubbed down with an insect repellent called Antimoustique, which had a very distinctive smell. On the very rare occasions I have come across that odour since, it immediately recalled that Belgian holiday. Another novelty that sticks in my mind was being taken to a Belgian hairdresser who, without asking, combed some kind of glue-like fixative into my hair. When I got home I was surprised to find that touching my hair felt like touching a gramophone record. It was like a solid helmet. Combing it was totally impossible but also quite unnecessary. That advantage wore off after a few days, however. Once forcibly lifted, any tuft stuck up like an antenna.

Of our many excursions, perhaps the most memorable was to the big harbour of Zeebrugge when a huge liner of the White Star line was berthed and held an open day for the public. It was like a luxurious floating fairy tale city, with palatial dining rooms, rows of shops and a swimming pool. It left an impression which still resonates with me seventy years later.

What I did not realise at the time was that the end of my childhood was rapidly approaching. We children were excited to see Belgian planes overhead practising aerobatics and towing and machine-gunning aerial targets all day long. In retrospect I recollect that the string-bag biplanes looked like World War I fighters and would stand no chance against the modern Luftwaffe monoplanes. The signs of the approaching war – the black hole that would swallow us – were all around. I suppose the first intimations of the end of my childhood came when I realised that my mother was worried to death and, even though I did not understand the details, I felt her fear and black despair.

Hitler was about to annex the Sudeten, with the acquiescence of the West, and my father was not with us. He had gone back and was somewhere in Czechoslovakia. There was not only all our possessions, but also his father and sister Else, to be moved to what he then thought was safety, in Prague. So our holiday at Wenduine ended. I do not know whether my mother ran out of money but first we moved to a flat in Blankenberge, which still felt like part of a seaside holiday, and then we moved to Brussels, presumably to await the return of my father. My mother spent a lot of time on the telephone. My brother and I played in a large department store across the street, going up and down the escalators much of the day. That was the first department store we had ever seen and it occupied what passed for a skyscraper in those days, so there was any number of escalators for two small boys.

By that time it seemed out of the question that my father could travel across Germany by train to join us, but somehow he managed to get on an aeroplane. I believe the only airline flying the route from Brussels to Prague was Sabena and eventually my father flew into Brussels with return air tickets for us.

Here is another little episode that has stayed with me: at the time there were stories in the papers about a man being killed by walking into a rotating propeller of a stationary plane at the airport. When, after a long time of waiting, my father phoned to say he had landed and was coming to collect us, my mother was greatly relieved. After all the disappointments she had, I must have been concerned that she should not raise her hopes prematurely, so I said to her: 'Well, the only thing that can go wrong now is that he will walk into a propeller.' I got a very funny look from my mother. I suppose I remember that because it is a typical example of my always imagining the worst-case scenario, as a protective mechanism, and then feeling guilty for sharing it.

So my first experience of flying was in a Sabena eleven-seater corrugated metal Junkers tri-motor, the first precursor of modern airliners. They were not pressurised and flew through the weather at low altitude. We probably flew close to its ceiling height because war was imminent and no-one was sure the Germans would not shoot down planes crossing their territory. I was terrified because we were being bumped up and down. I was sitting opposite the cabin altimeter and whenever we sank through a turbulence air hole for what seemed like a mile I was amazed that it registered no more that a quiver of the needle. So we landed in Prague.

Just to set the chronology straight, Hitler annexed the Sudeten in early October 1938. I had to start school again on 7

September and that would have been one reason for having to return. Czechoslovakia was not invaded until March 1939.

My father had rented a house on the outskirts of Prague – Smíchov, Na Černém Vrchu ('On the Black Hill'). The house was a villa of two storeys with a garage. The garage was essential because whatever furniture my father managed to transport from Aussig that did not fit into the new, much more modest, accommodation had to be stored. My aunt Else and my paternal grandfather, Karl, who must have been in his eighties then, lived upstairs and we lived in the downstairs flat. My brother and I, having flown on a real airplane recently, played airports on my grandfather's bald head, which he seemed to enjoy as much as we did. We took our meals together with my mother doing the cooking. I do not think my aunt was enamoured of cooking; fashion and making herself look beautiful were more in Else's line.

Aunt Else had always been an exception to the ladies of my mother's acquaintance. She was divorced, and she was very elegant, tall and slim, like my father. There is a tragic end to her story, as to so many others. She met a very charming young man and, as I found out after the war, they must have actually got married after we left. Else was eventually stuck in Prague, as she alone was left to look after her father. They were deported to Terezín together where my grandfather died and she was then moved to Auschwitz. After my liberation and return to Prague, I bumped into her man, who turned up in uniform as an Allied soldier in the Israeli Brigade, having fought alongside the

British forces, and he asked if I knew anything of her fate. By that time he was extremely ill with what I assumed to be heart disease. I remember walking with him to the refugee office and having to stop every hundred yards or so for him to catch his breath. He died shortly afterwards.

So Prague was my fourth permanent residence by the time I was eleven years old. As with the others, it involved huge changes in my circumstances. Our villa was on the flat top of a hill where a square, grass-covered common was surrounded by houses on all but one side, the fourth side giving onto a steep, wooded rocky slope that led down to the Smíchov suburbs. I started at a new school, too. On the way there I would pass the Bertramka, a little hollow lane up a steep hill flanking the Mozarteum, a famous landmark and place of pilgrimage for today's tourists.

There was no piano in our new abode, but since learning some music was always considered an essential part of my education, I had cello lessons from my uncle who was Professor of the Cello at the Prague Conservatoire. He had changed his name from Altschul to Alt and was married to his cousin Hilde. As befitted his elevated standing in the music world, he was rather impatient as the teacher of a small clumsy boy and tended to rap me over my knuckles with his bow when I got the fingering wrong. But all this was just a brief interlude.

3

The End of Hope

My father left for England via Holland to make a new life for us there. He must have departed at night so as not to upset us children but, given his frequent travels, we did not find his absence unusual. To this day I do not know the date of his departure. Having found employment in England, he proceeded to obtain papers to enable us to emigrate. Meanwhile it became clear that Hitler intended to attack Czechoslovakia; but we were going to fight! My patriotic fervour peaked during a national holiday (probably the twentieth anniversary of the founding of the republic) when our school assembled, along with many other schools and crowds of adults, in a huge stadium at Petřín – opposite where we lived in Smíchov. Hundreds of children formed an outline of the country and acted out various significant events in the development of the Czechoslovak Republic, including an early attack by the Hungarians, accompanied by much gunfire and rousing music. The spirit of the crowd swept me off my feet. Such nationalist enthusiasm was evidence that we were definitely going to fight the Germans (with myself in the forefront, at the age of eleven). The expectation was not, I think, that we had any chance of defeating the massive German military machine alone, but in those heady times we believed the civilised world would rush to help because it could not afford to allow that fairest star in the democratic constellation to be extinguished without deadly peril to itself.

So the Munich sell-out was an unbelievable disappointment. My recollection is that Hitler summoned President Hácha to Berlin (Beneš having fled to London) and he was not allowed to leave before agreeing that Bohemia and Moravia should become a German Protectorate. Germany invaded Czechoslovakia in March 1939. We did not go to downtown Prague to watch the troops marching in, but there was no way of ignoring the great formations of German bombers droning overhead in swastika formations.

Then came the hardest time for my mother. I do not know and do not even want to speculate about whether my father allowed for her inexperience in handling officialdom, but I have her, almost daily and increasingly desperate, letters to him. He had arranged Red Cross transportation to England for the three of us, but there is some mystery I cannot fathom regarding the required travel documents. My mother found she lacked certain items, such as birth certificates, which may have been mislaid. During the period from March to August her letters speak of missing documents, hundreds of people queuing, things 'not being as easy as he imagines', her inability to sleep without medication and eventually the dread the family would never be

Photographs of my brother and myself taken in Prague after my father's departure.

reunited. Finally, when we turned up at Gestapo headquarters in Prague with our suitcases packed ready to leave for England, we were turned back. I believe that we were in the first group to be refused travel. By 3 September, the war had started. I imagine that, along with her despair and self-reproach, I detect a note of relief in my mother's last letters, when matters had been taken out of her hands. She sent my father professionally taken photographs of my brother and myself to show him how much we had grown during his absence (see previous page).

My father was undoubtedly good at arranging things. All his life he shielded my mother from having to act on her own. Often the discovery of one's aptitude emerges only when one is amazed and irritated by someone else's inadequacy in that field. I suspect that marriages and relationships suffer when people try to change each other, and it is especially sad when the differences between them once seemed so endearing. My father may have treated my mother as a darling little scatterbrain, but that was a token of his affection and mainly due to his masculine tendency to take control. It should hardly have come as a great surprise that she found it difficult to cope once circumstances made huge and unusual demands on her. The dreadful penalty our family paid for such foibles seems unjustly extreme.

While these tragic events led to our being stuck in what became the Protectorate of Bohemia and Moravia, with my father on the other side of the Channel in England, I went to school, passed all my exams for secondary education, practised the cello and fell massively in love for the first time. Hanka Klei-nová had long dark hair, the most perfect complexion, and was altogether the most beautiful being on God's earth. I once thought I detected a blemish on her face and prayed I had been mistaken. Sex did not enter into it; had she offered to kiss me, I believe I would have run a mile. I may have been a troubadour in a previous incarnation.

Eventually my mother ran out of money so we could not stay on in the Prague flat. We parted with my aunt and grandfather. I met Tante Else once more in Terezín but my grandfather had died by that time. In the meantime, we were taken in by the family of Rudolf Pick in Ústí nad Orlicí (Wildenschwert; by way of explaining the proliferation of *Ústís*, 'Ústí' is Czech for a river mouth or confluence). So that was the fifth move of my short existence but another contribution to my survival, since deportations from the small towns took place substantially later than those from Prague.

Rudolf Pick was not really my uncle; my mother was distantly related to his wife, 'Aunt' Fanny (born Fantl). I had met the Pick family several years before. They had two children: Alice, who died before the war, aged about twenty, from a tuberculosis infection which spread to her eye, and her younger brother Fredy, who was in his late teens. To my childish eyes they all looked enormously fat and were evidently very rich.

Uncle Pick, owned a glove factory at the edge of town close to the small river and must have been a major employer of the townspeople. There is still a street named after his father, Julius.

The Picks visiting us during our holidays. Adults from the right: Fredy, Rudolph and Fanny Pick. Their chauffeur and his wife on the left, my parents centre.

The family travelled in a huge chauffeur-driven Tatra car. I do not think any of them could drive. My uncle's house at 123 Rašínova seemed like a castle to me. After all, it did have a sort of turret and heavy wrought-iron gates as well as a large veranda at the back and a big garden with four great pine trees in its centre.

The elegant rooms downstairs were heated by huge Dutch stoves made of polished silvery metal with mica windows through which the flames were visible. Incidentally, it was through these windows that I discovered the existence of false teeth. My uncle had a liking for toffees. Having bitten into one, it evidently stuck the upper set to the lower, whereupon he decided to get rid of the offending sweet by furtively opening the door of the stove and spitting, inadvertently ejecting his dentures. It must have been the spectacular deflagration which followed and brightly illuminated my embarrassed uncle's toothlessness that fixed the event in my memory. I believe false teeth were made of highly flammable nitrocellulose in those days, as were toothbrushes.

The bath was a miniature swimming pool with three steps leading into it. The fuel consumption of the boiler which heated the bathwater was such that, once shortages begun to bite, bath night came only once a week and accommodated everybody, with the three Weinbergs sharing the same bathwater. I do not suppose such arrangements applied before the war.

To begin with, before the Germans got their anti-Jewish laws organised, life in the grand house was fairly normal. Although I had passed all the entrance exams for the Gymnasium (grammar school) in Prague, no such institution was available locally so I went to the secondary school just across the road, which was the equivalent of a secondary modern, a profoundly unpleasant place where, again, children were beaten – me included this time. There was an old arts teacher and each of his classes started with the children who had not done their homework ceremonially queuing up to be beaten in a little cubicle. I turned up for my first week there when the school term was already underway, so I had no opportunity to do the homework and did not know what was expected of me. When it was my turn, I was duly ordered to bend over a desk and was beaten with a strap. I assumed that the right thing to do on returning to the classroom was to display an air of nonchalance rather than show distress or, heaven forfend, tears. Not my idea of education, but character-building in an upper-lip-stiffening sort of way nonetheless. Beating children was the only distinction the establishment shared with English public schools.

More and more of the anti-Jewish laws were implemented in the Czech protectorate, and I was thrown out of school at the end of the academic year, the only good idea the Nazis ever hit on. And that was the end of the only conventional school education I ever had.

One or two members of the Jewish community made an effort to teach me whatever they remembered from their own school days. My particular favourite was Mr Kauder, a bachelor who lived with his old mother and a dove that spent its life in a cage and, every now and again, laid a tiny egg. The egg was then hard-boiled by old Mrs Kauder and ceremoniously halved and shared between her and her son. Mr Kauder gave me lessons in a distinctly odd set of subjects. I instantly took to logarithms, including the use of a slide rule (which brought home to me that long multiplication and division are for suckers) and coordinate geometry. He also tried to teach me to sketch, though I had little aptitude and could only learn a few artist's tricks. I started to play the violin, but I never had long enough on any instrument (other than the harmonica) to become proficient.

I found this lack of proficiency frustrating because the Pick family were very gifted musically. Before the war there were regular performances in the dining room. Both my aunt and my mother were accomplished pianists and my uncle's violin playing was good enough for some of the internationally famous Czech violinists to visit occasionally and to join in their chamber music concerts. Uncle Pick and my mother were also talented graphic artists and produced our little community's own newspaper. I think they got quite fond of each other, to the point of making aunt Fanny jealous.

My aunt was an unhappy soul. She never recovered from the first tragedy of daughter Alice's death and now made daily pilgrimages to the cemetery accompanied by her two dachshunds, both called Waldi. The Waldis were given our dinner plates to lick clean at the end of every meal. Waldi senior had eye and ear infections and smelled to high heaven. Bearing in mind the near sterile conditions under which we had been brought up, our reaction to this lack of hygiene may well be imagined. Nothing was said, of course, as we were house guests.

Aunt Fanny was pretty massive, with the agility of a hippopotamus. When she entered the swimming pool, the urchins shouted: 'High water – everyone out!' She had quite a reputation as a cook, based on her inventive use of unpromising raw materials. I cannot remember whether we dreaded her bread soup more than her milk soup. She made her own cheese by allowing strained milk curds to moulder in tureens which were distributed over the tops of all the wardrobes and harvested in chronological order. A variation on the theme involved boiling the ripe mixture, which resulted in a product with the appearance and taste of glue and vinegar. All that aroma added unforgettably to the ambience of the household. My mother, brother and I shared a double bed in a small room (including a porcelain cold-water jug and a washbasin). We felt so homesick for our former life we often cried ourselves to sleep.

As the new German anti-Jewish regulations were enforced, our quality of life deteriorated very rapidly. All the domestic staff had to leave – some departing very reluctantly and afterwards coming to visit at night. Long lists of executed townspeople (many for listening to the BBC) were posted regularly outside the town hall. In due course we had to sew the *Judenstern* – the yellow Star of David – onto our coats and jackets. Then my treasured bicycle and our skis were confiscated. The authorities did not get round to confiscating skates, however, and, as we had an exceptionally cold winter that year, the snow froze so hard we could skate in the streets. We children could, that is; the adults' lesser power-to-weight ratio made it too hard on their ankles.

I did actually have my Bar Mitzvah in April 1941, the preparation for which required me to take instruction from a Rabbi in a nearby town. The prohibition preventing Jews from travelling came into force shortly after my thirteenth birthday.

One of the consequences of not being allowed to go to school and the many other successive restrictions was that we had a great deal of spare time. I got to know every path in the beautiful forests on the surrounding hills. Sometimes the whole family went on fungi-collecting expeditions, and I became expert in finding and recognising edible fungi. On our trail, when we had the time and strength, we could climb to the peak of the mountain, where there was (and still is) a chalet, which sold bread thickly spread with real butter to selected customers, long after butter was just a memory in the town. More often my brother and I were out in the woods and meadows looking down on the roofs of the small town. We spent days doing nothing but walk, with me telling him unending stories that I made up as I went along. As far as I can remember, they cast us in the roles of famous athletes, musicians, racing drivers (famous *whatevers*) and the adventures that befell as we toured the world. No one ever spoke to us, perhaps because people were afraid to be seen alongside our yellow stars. Whatever the explanation, we never experienced any unkindness from the local Czechs.

Food shortages worsened due, I suppose, to requisitioning for the German army. I had been the little boy who used to complain, 'Only dry bread with butter?' when there was nothing more interesting to eat, and now there was not enough bread, whilst butter had become a scarce delicacy. So somebody came up with the brilliant idea of sending me to work on a farm. My uncle knew the farmer who, I believe, used to supply the family with fresh eggs, butter and poultry, in happier days. There would be one less mouth to feed at home and I would benefit from plentiful farm food. The farmer, on the other hand, saw it as an opportunity to acquire an unpaid farmhand; it was clearly a recipe for disappointment all round.

I was dispatched to the farm in a small village nearby, Sloup-
nice. The main problem was that I had never done a day's hard
physical labour in my life – quite unlike the country boys my
own age. I was also totally unprepared for how primitive the life
of the Czech peasant was at that time. Flails were used for
threshing, scythes for harvesting and a horse-drawn, wooden-
wheeled cart for conveying loads too heavy to carry.

My first and crucial mistake was to ignore advice to keep my
shirt on. That summer we had scorching days and nightly thunderstorms. I was put in charge of an implement like a small
plough, which, instead of a ploughshare, had two blades that cut
roots of weeds under the soil when pushed hard enough between
rows of crops. (After the war I spotted such a device in a museum
of ancient agricultural implements.) I felt sure the contraption
had been designed to be pulled by a horse but, since the horse
was otherwise engaged, I was obliged to do the work on its
behalf. A day's weeding between rows of potato plants resulted
in aching muscles and a severely sunburned back. Since I had to
sleep on a bag of straw, I had all and every night to rue my
stupidity.

My bed was in a corridor separating the farm building from
the stables. If I needed to empty my bladder, it was only a few
steps to the cow shed. There were no doors and no light, so
stepping into a cowpat before returning to bed was not an
uncommon experience. The absence of doors also allowed the
wind to howl through the passage during the nightly thunderstorms, cooling my burnt back with a fine spray of rainwater.

Breakfast consisted of mashed potatoes in a big bowl. The correct procedure, I quickly learned, was to take a big spoonful of mash, dip it into a communal bowl of milk, then into a plate of granular sugar, before shoving it into one's mouth, along with the shared saliva of all around the table. All this was a major culture shock to me – but no one went hungry. I lasted about a week, during which I decided I was not cut out to be a peasant, though I was left with the mastery of scything. Swinging the blade at the correct angle for cutting the stalks, the one activity which gave me satisfaction, proved of limited applicability in my subsequent career as an academic.

So, after a single inglorious week, I returned to my uncle's house as a failed farm hand. One of the few people we could visit on our outings was Mr Perlhaefter, Jewish but married to a gentile, who lived right on the lovely cobbled square at the centre of the small town. He was a spare-time organist and wrote church music, which, in a happier era, half the Jewish community went to hear when it was performed in the great church. He became the sole survivor of the indigenous Jewish community. Because he was married to a gentile he was deported much later than the rest of us and only as far as Terezín. Having sworn to wear the yellow Star of David if he survived he had a replica made in the form of a small enamelled pin, which he wore to the end of his life. He must have been responsible for the memorial in the cemetery commemorating all the deceased Jews of Ústí, which I saw after the war. He was also the keeper of my few surviving possessions, including my precious family photo album, which he hid along with a number of other people's personal effects during the war in case there were any survivors.

Time was rapidly running out for the little Jewish community. About a dozen individuals who lived in the upper part of the town had to move into my uncle's house, which was just about big enough to accommodate us all. In the autumn of 1942 that house was requisitioned by the German administration and we all had to move into the tiny flat of the Weiners, a retired couple, who lived opposite the church. There were many of us to each room and we had to sleep on mattresses scattered across the floor. I ended up on a pile of blankets when we ran out of mattresses.

We knew we were about to be deported with only what each of us could carry in one suitcase. The matter was not discussed with us children, but we had anti-typhus shots, which made us very feverish, and we witnessed watches and valuable items of jewellery being hidden in tins of shoe polish. The valuables were embedded in Plasticene on the base of the emptied tin, covered with a false bottom, and then the tin was topped up with molten shoe polish. Oddly enough, the grown-ups allowed for the likelihood that the contents would be probed with prongs but not for the much more probable contingency that the luggage would simply be confiscated. Incidentally, I have often wondered whether somebody got a wonderful surprise when using up the last of a tin of boot polish many years later.

It was not long before a Wehrmacht detachment with bayonets fixed came knocking on doors to herd us onto the special train waiting for us at the station. There was a delay while the supervising SS officer sent soldiers to collect one old couple who had not turned up as directed. I was not looking forward to seeing how they would be treated but they never appeared, having taken an overdose the night before. In the years that followed I came to think of that as a sort of victory.

PART II

The Camps

4

Holocaust Literature and Reality

I never intended to write about the camps, partly because I tried hard to forget; I wanted to live for the future and not define myself as 'a camp survivor'. I have always tended to avoid Holocaust literature, and find some of the recent fictional accounts masquerading as true stories profoundly disturbing. Falsifying history to make a more marketable story is nothing new, of course, and so long as the result is presented as fiction there is no harm; but it so often is not. Were I a descendant of Salieri, I should, no doubt, resent the widespread belief that my ancestor poisoned Mozart. For that matter, I am as cross as any true-bred Englishman that a recent film falsely attributes the capture of the crucial Enigma machine to the Americans.

None of this compares to the repugnance that fabricated Holocaust stories induce in me and the few fellow survivors with whom I remain in contact. To us it is tantamount to desecrating war graves. Almost seventy shipwrecks and all underwater military aircraft are protected as war graves under the Protection of Military Remains Act of 1986; plundering them is an offence.

That is an expression of the nation's respect for some thousands of brave souls who gave their lives in a cause worth dying for. Here we are talking about many millions, mostly children, women and men too old or sick to work, who died at the whim of a deranged mind. We ought at least to show them enough respect to refrain from making up false stories about the way their lives ended.

History is necessarily written by the survivors, but at its core it is the story of the victims. It is always liable to distortion because anyone who survived the extermination camps must have an untypical story to tell. The typical camp history of the millions ended in death, and could therefore never be told in the first person. In my case, it was only a most improbable succession of many unlikely turns of almost miraculous good fortune that allowed my story to see the light of day but the least I can do is to speak up truthfully for those who did not make it.

There is another reason why my narrative cannot be a detailed continuous diary. In the camps I tried to acquire the ability to look without seeing, listen without hearing and smell without taking in what was around me. I cultivated a kind of self-induced amnesia. I feared that being made to look at hangings, seeing piles of corpses on a daily basis, would somehow contaminate my mind permanently. To quote George Bernard Shaw (from *Man and Superman* – not that I had read it then): 'Better keep yourself clean and bright, for you are the window through which you must see the world.' We probably all have the latent ability to prevent horrific memories becoming fixed in the brain's synapses. After all, we pull off the same trick every morning when we forget our dreams. The downside is that the habit of wilfully forgetting may become involuntary.

The authoritative history of the camps is well documented; it is now possible to Google most of the facts (though not all the entries are equally reliable). What a camp survivor alone can convey is what it felt like. For example, most people know what it is like to have a horrific nightmare and the relief of waking to reality. Few, I think, can imagine the converse: waking from wonderful dreams of happy childhood to the nightmare of reality, the reek of bodies crowded either side – the realisation of where one is – night after night, week after week, month after month.

Strangely, a consoling thought was that even if one died from having one's face ground into the mud by a jackboot, death would be the same as for all those millions who died in peacetime, in the comfort of their feather beds. Who would have thought that falling into and being covered in mud could lead to despondency such as to destroy one's will to live, whilst a painful blow from a rifle butt might be so infuriating as to have exactly the opposite effect?

One of the side effects of intermittent self-induced amnesia is that it tends to disrupt and distort the flow of time. Some episodes seemed to last an eternity, whereas others were over in a flash. The chronology of my major moves is set out in an appendix (there is an uncertainty in some of the dates but only to the extent of a day or two either side).

5

Ghetto Theresienstadt (Terezín)

The train took us to Pardubice, some fifty kilometres east of Ústí nad Orlicí. Pardubice is the district capital and has several halls with enough floor space to sleep large numbers. I must admit I was actually quite excited about the adventure, after many months of boredom. I hadn't spoken to another teenager since I left school. Now there were actually *girls* there, and of my own age, background and religion. I thought I looked very smart in a dark-green outfit made from my father's ski suit. We slept on mats on the floor in a large hall in the collection centre. However, being so close to my brand-new acquaintances had repercussions. I contracted scarlet fever and so did my brother.

The onset must have involved a high fever because I remember nothing of our arrival and reception in Terezín. My next recollection is of finding myself in bed in a children's ward of a hospital, where we had our heads shaved. I did not think that improved my appearance, vanity having reasserted itself by then, so I improvised a turban, which I decorated with my mother's polar bear-shaped silver brooch. Under Terezín's crowded conditions, serial epidemics spread rapidly. During my time there, many children contracted scarlet fever and later polio. In the bed next to mine was a tiny child whose breathing sounded like the crumpling of a paper bag. He died of pneumonia a few days after my admission. Up to that time I had only ever seen one corpse; as a small boy I once caught a glimpse of the bloated body of a man who drowned in the Vltava and had been dragged out onto the towpath. The sight affected me profoundly and from then on I tried never to kill any living creature, if I could avoid it. Never again did I incinerate ants with a magnifying glass.

What would have surprised me most, though I did not find out until after the war, was that Terezín was located barely thirty kilometres from my birth place, Ústí nad Labem, in the northeast corner of Bohemia and not far from the Elbe river of my happy childhood. Terezín had been built as a moated and walled fort, star-shaped in plan form, full of solid multistoried garrison buildings. It had been built in the late eighteenth century by Emperor Joseph II, who named it for his mother, Maria Theresa of Austria.

The garrison was probably intended for some 7,000 soldiers, whilst the ghetto inhabitants must have numbered almost ten times as many. This allowed about two square metres of floor space per person. Every room was congested with triple-tiered bunk beds, which left little provision for private possessions. Although we were deeply shocked by the shortage of food and individual living space, Terezín was survivable with a bit of luck, though tens of thousands did not.

Terezín was nothing like an extermination or slave labour camp. It was a holding pen for Auschwitz and the like, and also served the Nazis as a showcase for inspections from the Red Cross. We were allowed to keep our clothes and hair (once it re-grew, following our discharge from the hospital). There was an element of self-government. There were Jewish policemen wearing hats modelled on those of the French police. There was the *Judenrat*, a Jewish council charged with the apocalyptic task of selecting people for deportation to the death camps, fulfilling quotas set by the Nazis.

The main preoccupation in Terezín was to find 'protected' employment – a job recognized to be of sufficient importance to exempt a worker from transportation to the east. I had no idea what was in store for us in those camps and have often wondered if anyone did. Indeed, I frequently overheard grown-ups say, 'It couldn't possibly be much worse than here!' (How ludicrous that seems in retrospect.) But despite the ignorance surrounding it, transportation was a fate to be avoided, or at least deferred, if at all possible. My mother took up nursing, which gave us a whole year, without which I would not have survived to chronicle this history.

There were to be major consequences to my having been initiated into life in Terezín by way of a stay in a hospital. Children of my age went to school to continue with their education. However, by the time I was discharged, I had missed that opportunity and had to join the workforce. I have sometimes wondered whether the rapid blossoming of my postwar career had anything to do with this conspiracy of fate to deny me any formal education between the ages of twelve and seventeen. My brother, however, did go to school.

Terezín boasted a flourishing cultural life. The place was, after all, full of prominent artists, writers, musicians, and distinguished intellectuals of every kind. The school itself put on stage performances; there were concerts, cabarets and even sports and athletics activities. A running track and sports ground were laid out on top of one of the corner ramparts. I did well in the sprint and discus, though I am not convinced it was a sensible activity for undernourished teenagers. Tickets to all the concerts and shows were in great demand and eagerly sought after. I mention this because, much as I try to avoid reading some of the nonsense that is written on this subject, I came across the statement in someone's PhD thesis that 'inmates were forced to attend these performances to impress visiting Red Cross delegations' – a gratuitous inference which defies both fact and common sense.

My first job in Terezín was as a medical assistant in a clinic. I learned to wind and apply bandages and to lance abscesses, essential skills since outbreaks of boils were frequent. We had a very limited supply of pharmaceuticals but I applied much gentian violet and zinc ointment to infected wounds. *Bolus alba* was a pharmaceutical generally plentiful in the camps. While writing this, I became curious and looked up the medical uses of that white powder which is, in fact, Kaolin. Here it is: 'Orally, kaolin is used for mild to moderate acute diarrhoea, cholera, enteritis, and dysentery. Topically, kaolin is used as a poultice, dusting powder, drying agent, and emollient.' This is obviously ideal stuff to stock up on, for both internal and topical use, for anyone intent on running concentration camps on a restricted budget. In Buchenwald it was used in vast quantities following the amputation of frostbitten toes.

My job took a turn for the worse when the polio epidemic struck and I became a stretcher-bearer. Not only was that very heavy outdoor work, but the risk of contracting polio was real and terrifying. I did not, in fact, catch it: I got jaundice (hepatitis A, I suppose) instead. Epidemics of various kinds were rife because of the crowded conditions, though the illnesses tended to be less severe in consequence. The jaundice left me with a life-long intolerance of alcohol and nausea when confronted with rotten potatoes. I must have eaten some during the onset of the illness; I doubt there was a causal connection.

The following spring it was decided I was too young for the work I had been assigned (I had, after all, just turned fifteen), and I became a member of a juvenile gardening team. The outer ramparts of the fort were under soil and had been converted to vegetable gardens. My team worked under the supervision of a Mr Karplus, a professional gardener. In good weather it was a hard but pleasant outdoor occupation which, moreover, offered useful training and the opportunity of smuggling out the occasional head of cabbage, if one felt brave enough to stroll past the guards looking improbably pregnant.

For much of the time I slept in a dormitory for boys aged fourteen to eighteen. I shared a middle bunk bed with Walter, who was about two years older than I. Walter had an unfortunate habit of what would now be called 'inappropriate touching'. It was too tentative and gentle, I suppose, to be called abuse, but I hated it and kept telling him so. One day when we were dressing for work standing next to the bed, I got so furious when he tried to grope me that I hit him in the face with such force he fell backward into a clothes rack. He did not try to retaliate, even though he was quite a lot bigger. That was the end of his efforts to seduce me but also the end of any communication between us. In retrospect, I felt sorry for his bad luck in having drawn a sleeping companion who happened to be at the opposite extreme end of the sexual spectrum, and also totally uninterested in sex under the circumstances. I always seem to have been attractive to homosexuals though – which turned out later to be yet another factor in saving my life.

My best friend on a purely intellectual level was Kurt, a gangling eighteen-year-old poet, a devotee of Hegel's philosophy, who had little time for washing or shaving and tended to be bullied by the others in the dormitory. He was double my height but the bullying was not physical. The fact that I wanted to read what he had written and listened earnestly to his philosophising clearly was a comfort to him.

I had yet one more medical emergency before leaving Terezín. It came about as the result of a deeply frustrated desire for some little private space to store a few small treasured possessions. I was trying to chisel out a cubbyhole, no larger than one brick, just above my head in the bunk bed. I was encouraged by the ease of penetrating the first one or two inches of plaster, when I hit solid rock. Thereafter it was very hard going and, as I kept chiselling, I suddenly felt a blow as if something had hit my eye. I thought no more about it until I developed a persistent eye inflammation. Now, it may come as a surprise to those who write conjecture-based theses about Terezín that it was possible to go to a competent eye surgeon there and have a granite splinter that had penetrated the cornea removed under a local anaesthetic. Later, in the Auschwitz camps, of course, one never admitted to being ill, in case one got sent to the gas chambers. To this day, whenever I have an eye examination, I am always asked how I came by the deep gash in my eye (I then have to say, 'That is rather a long story').

I visited my mother whenever I could. On one occasion we went together to meet Aunt Else and sat under a tree in fine drizzle – it was a sad meeting. She had been deported from Prague with her father long before us and grandfather had died some time before our arrival. I consoled myself with the thought that at least he lived to a ripe old age. That was also the last time I saw Aunt Else; she was deported to Auschwitz on the next transport and I do not know what happened to her.

My mother was not, I suppose, conventionally beautiful (unlike Aunt Else, incidentally, who was noted for her good looks), but she had great personality and vivacity and was never short of male admirers. Her first Terezín friend was a baker by profession. Working as a fully qualified baker in a bakery was protected employment. I suppose there was no shortage of doctors, lawyers, and other middle-class professionals but Jewish bakers were at a premium. Getting up at some unearthly hour of the morning to shovel loaves into a hot oven – what kind of job is that for a nice Jewish boy? I did not think much of him because I considered him too old and ugly for my wonderful mother but he kept coming up with the odd loaf of bread for us. I suspect that my mother kept up the friendship for our sake.

In due course my mother became a nurse in a mental hospital. Psychiatric nursing was also protected, at least to begin with. Unsurprisingly, there were a great many mentally disturbed patients, who were hospitalised in tunnel-shaped wards under the rampart beyond the moat. I visited the smelly wards which became my mother's sphere of activity just once and never allowed myself to repeat the experience. She became friendly with a male colleague; he may even have been instrumental in my mother getting the job in the first place. He was an interesting character; an admirer of Stoicism as a philosophy, who believed that mankind's greatest strength lay in our ability to commit suicide when life became intolerable. He was deported to Auschwitz six months before we were, yet he did not kill himself until my mother turned up there. I believe I came to understand how his pride made the act inescapable.

I wondered subsequently why occupations such as psychiatric nursing, which initially conferred protection from transportation, eventually ceased to do so. One took it for granted that members of the *Judenrat*, police, and other high officials, would be exempt, so long as they remained in office. Since all such organisations tend to proliferate, eventually people at the edge of the protected sphere of employment had to be sacrificed. I have no justification for this conjecture, other than my experience of how administrative hierarchies burgeon.

Those selected for transportation were first corralled into a parade ground which formed the centre of each of the multi-storey garrison buildings. It was possible for friends to wave and shout messages from the upper-storey gangways, but the ground floor was isolated by Wehrmacht guards. In due course, that became our lot. After almost a year in Terezín, our time was up and we were escorted to the cattle trucks of the train to Auschwitz.

6

Auschwitz-Birkenau

I regard that journey very much as part of the Auschwitz, not the Terezín, experience. It was pitch black inside the truck – mid December and no windows. I think there were too many of us for all to sit down. My instinct was to head for a wall and sit down with my back against it (but there is guilt associated with every survival manoeuvre; if I sit, someone else has to stand and be tossed about).

How do people behave when squashed into railway cattle trucks en route to Auschwitz? If they wailed and moaned, I did not hear, and I suppose their immediate neighbours would have turned on them. We had no idea, of course, what was in store for us – at least I did not. Those around me were cuddling and making love, as far as I could tell in the dark. I don't know whether they were family, friends, or total strangers; it is in any case the most life-affirming activity and I felt rather left out. I wish I had known then how to meditate. I called out to my mother and brother – we got separated by the soldiers who were herding us – and to my great relief I discovered they were sitting in the same truck, some distance away.

When at last we arrived and were ejected onto the ramp, I was blinded by arc lights slicing through the murk. There was a reception committee of large and ugly SS men to herd us. Some had sticks, some had large and terrifying Alsatian dogs on leads, some had both; all had the death's head (*Totenkopf*) insignia on their caps. At least mediaeval paintings of hell portrayed it as a warm place! (There are a few German commands to which I still have an immediate visceral aversion. They are 'Schnell! Schnell!' and 'Rauss! Rauss!' in particular. I'm not that keen on *Schweinehund* either.)

A great many acts of barbaric cruelty were perpetrated in Auschwitz; not all of them by the guards. The Kapos also had powers of life or death over us. They were in charge of individual barracks, in which they had their own small rooms. They tended to carry big sticks, wore riding boots and had been in Auschwitz for a long time. Many of them were criminals on sabbatical from the dregs of German jails. (*Schwerverbrecher* does not translate well into English but I imagine that psychopaths with a few sadistic murders on their CVs would have had a head start in the selection process for the job.)

Cruelty and brutality, however, were not Nazi inventions. The middle ages witnessed people being disembowelled, broken on wheels or burnt at the stake. The Nazi's unique and original contribution to man's inhumanity to man, however, was the industrialisation of genocide.

I became familiar with that assembly line system during my subsequent grand tour of Nazi concentration camps. The reception establishment was euphemistically (or perhaps ironically) called the 'sauna'. All possessions, clothes and shoes had to be dumped in the first room. One then proceeded to the shower room, which involved delousing, disinfecting, head shaving and, where appropriate for first-time arrivals, tattooing. In the last room one was issued with striped prison 'pyjamas' and footwear.

As the war progressed, the pyjamas became increasingly thinner, scratchier and the material more straw-like. The boots were made of canvas nailed to wooden soles. With luck, the outfit would not be completely the wrong size.

In the extermination camps there were similar establishments in which the showers dispensed not water but gas and there was no clothing in the last room. (This, clearly, is not recounted from personal experience, except for the knowledge that the victims were led to believe that they were going to the showers.)

However, for some reason I have never fully understood, our Auschwitz-Birkenau *Familienlager* (family camp) initiation routine was different. We kept our clothes and hair. I suspect it was because the camp was just a holding pen for the Czech Jews from Terezín scheduled to be liquidated in the gas chambers six months after arrival. It was, perhaps, just not worth the trouble of opening additional camps to separate men from women and children. An alternative theory I have been told is that the arrangement was to hoodwink the Red Cross, in case they decided to check on what happened to the Jews from Terezín. By gassing each transport after six months in the camp, there would always be a supply of the most recent arrivals to inspect, if necessary. The most significant privilege, from my point of view, was that men, women and children, though segregated in different barracks, were free to visit each other. Even the tattooing of numbers on our forearms was carried out later, by specialist teams of prisoners visiting individual barracks. Incidentally, the number in the title of this narrative is my Buchenwald, not my Auschwitz number. It seemed appropriate to count my adulthood from the liberation of Buchenwald when my life was given back to me and I ceased to be just that number.

There is probably no need to describe the layout of the Auschwitz-Birkenau camps. There can be few people in the world who have not seen the grim photographs of the adjacent narrow strips, each with a single street with long black wooden huts facing it at right angles, each strip enclosed by high voltage barbed wire fences and guard towers with searchlights and guns. What is not evident from photographs is the smell of mud mixed with calcium hypochlorite, particularly at the far end where the latrine and washroom (and, as it so happens, my barrack) were situated. Calcium hypochlorite is bleaching powder and its unique and penetrating stench will forever be associated in my subconscious with that place. The Nazis were terrified of epidemics and, clearly unconvinced that Aryan DNA would be respected as distinct by pathogens, prescribed piling on the cheap disinfectant.

We were split up: my mother was herded into a women's hut and my brother into the children's block with which I became associated later and which was nearly opposite mine. The fifteenth of December 1943 was a really grim day. I had no idea of the true nature of our new camp until we were given a nightmarish tutorial by the men from previous transports who already occupied much of the block to which I was assigned – having been allocated my place in a four-storey bunk. (A bookmark would have been useful since we were squashed together like sardines on each level.)

That was, in fact, the first time I learned about the existence of the gas chambers and the significance of seeing smoke from the chimney of the adjacent crematorium. Although, presumably it was not our turn for another six months, any admission of having fallen ill would curtail that stay of execution.

There was a great deal of advice and information volunteered by the old hands. Our sole possessions – a spoon and an aluminium container for soup – were best used as a pillow at night; there was nowhere else to keep anything and thieving did take place, I am sorry to say. The term *Muselman* referred to any inmate who, having lost the will to live, just shuffled along, having given up on everything, including personal hygiene; since that entailed washing in the freezing washroom trough, using ice-cold water, it did require determination and will-power, especially in sub-zero December temperatures.

The thing to do when hit in the face by a guard was to fall down and stay down. With a bit of luck one would then not be hit again. I assumed that all German boys were brought up on the enormously popular Wild West books of Karl May; they were apparently some of Hitler's favourites. The German hero was called Old Shatterhand because of his ability to knock out any opponent with a single blow to the head. I was sure the SS men fancied themselves in that role.

My attitude to those SS thugs became a mixture of fear, contempt and revulsion. I could not really hate or judge them because they were not human by my standards. I am reminded of warning notices displayed near groups of Japanese apes in Japan's national parks which advise that looking the males in the eyes is regarded as a challenge and likely to cause them to attack. I dared not look our guards in the face in case they saw the contempt in my eyes – they could beat or kill us on a whim, so there was little point in provocation. At some level I suppose it had dawned even on the most thuggish among them that those emaciated shuffling Muselmen over whom they had dominion included the former intellectual elite of Europe. Perhaps that enhanced their job satisfaction. After all, did not one of their great leaders 'reach for his gun whenever he heard the word culture'? The 'Master Race' appeared to have mutated into an aberrant subspecies of hominid – the authentic Untermensch – a bizarre development in twentieth-century Europe!

In spite of my exhaustion on the day of arrival, I did not expect to sleep after this introduction to my new way of life. Nonetheless, I must have slept some of the night since I did not hear Kurt, my poetic friend and Hegel devotee, hang himself. He was in the same bunk and was hanging by his belt from its corner post when I was woken early in the morning for the roll call. My shock and sorrow was tinged by profound respect; I would not have expected such resolve from my bookish, philosophical friend.

I do not know how many other suicides occurred that night. Next morning I saw piles of corpses for the first time. Actually it was not that easy to kill oneself, even allowing for the apparently obvious method of grabbing the high-tension barbed wire fence. The run-up to it was not level ground; there was a shallow ditch and the posts were set on somewhat raised soil. Much later I saw blackened corpses hanging from the wire in Gross-Rosen (more of which later) but in our Familienlager one was never out of sight of the watchtowers or beyond the reach of their searchlights at night. Since we assumed that, at that stage of the war, any soldier of the Wehrmacht who was able to shoot at all straight would be at the front, the probability was that one would end up in the gas chamber with some not quite lethal bullet wounds – not an appealing way to go!

My mother tried for the Auschwitz Women's Orchestra, which conferred protection from the gas chambers and forced labour, but without success. I suppose there was a glut of amateur pianists – a common enough accomplishment among former middle-class ladies of leisure. She contracted meningitis during an epidemic sweeping the camp but again, very fortunately, it was generally not a serious illness there and one tended to keep very quiet about being ill. She was, of course, deeply depressed and no longer expected to survive the war.

I am not sure how much she blamed herself; that would have been a taboo subject between us, but she kept quoting an old German song or poem, repeating, 'It would have been too wonderful – it was not meant to be,' in relation to our family's future. However, she said to me on several occasions, 'If any of us survive, it will be you.' I am making myself record this harrowing tale to honour her memory.

My brother was allocated a place in the children's block, the existence and creation of which was a miracle made possible by one Fredy Hirsch. I do not know whether there may be a category of Jewish homosexual saints, but Fredy Hirsch deserves to be canonized for the many wonders he performed (including giving me a job which helped save my life) and he was martyred in the end. Fredy Hirsch was a German Jew who spoke in a clipped Aachen accent. He had been a teacher and organiser of youth sports activities already before the war. He was very active in the school system during his time in Terezín, though I had never met him before Birkenau. In the camp he presented a strikingly well-dressed, athletic figure, his aquiline features and slicked down black hair complemented by elegant Nazi-style leather boots. To me he epitomized everything the Nazis would admire.

I have no idea how he came by his evidently considerable influence with the SS but he used it to greatest effect in establishing the children's block, of which he was Kapo or *Block Aelteste* (Block Elder? Block Senior?). This protected the children to a large extent from the brutalities of camp life, from roll calls in the cold, and theft. Without wishing to detract from Fredy Hirsch's achievements in any way, it must have dawned on the Nazi authorities that the brutal camp regime would be easier to enforce without having lots of traumatized children of all ages running about the place. Fredy organised suitable activities for the various age groups, including some indoor sports and play performances.

Hut 31, the children's block, was an oasis in the surrounding desolation. There was an area behind the Kapo's room, with a rudimentary counter for distributing food, which eventually became my domain. Fredy was scrupulous about enforcing personal hygiene (in particular, insisting on closely inspecting the cleanliness of boys' private parts, mine included). Hand-painted murals of scenes from Disney films and fairy tales decorated the walls. (Incidentally, it is only quite recently that I learnt more about the artist who created those murals – on reading her obituary in *The Times*. This talented painter was a girl selected by the notorious Dr Mengele to paint portraits of Gypsy prisoners because he felt that photographs did not adequately emphasise their 'racial characteristics'. In return for exaggerating the features he wanted to emphasise he saved her and her mother from the gas chamber. She became a well-known artist and died recently, in America, from natural causes.)

I did not live in the children's block but, in another life-saving turn of good fortune, was picked out by Fredy Hirsch to serve in the *Menagedienst*, which entailed carting barrels of soup and 'coffee' around the camp and ladling portions out to the inmates.

The soup barrels were huge and far too heavy for us undernourished teenagers to carry. There were four of us and we used two long poles, which we threaded through the down-turned handles on either side of the barrel. When the barrels were full, we were just about able to lift them and run a few steps before having to rest again. So we proceeded through the camp, ending up in block 31 to serve the children.

The soup tasted chiefly of hot water. The other constituents were largely root vegetables (the ones ending in 'nips', as in turnips, parsnips, etcetera, which I swore never to touch again if I survived) and dried vegetables such as strips of cabbage leaves, collectively known as *Stacheldraht* (barbed wire). The 'coffee', however, contributed to my survival. It had clearly never seen a single coffee bean but it did contain sugar. If one did not stir it too assiduously (and the ladle was not long enough to reach base until most of the liquid had been dispensed), there would be left at the bottom of the container a mess of ersatz coffee consisting of chicory grounds and sugar, which we spooned out and shared among us carriers. The taste was revolting but it was full of calories – probably more in a day's helping than in a week's supply of the camp food. I doubt I would have survived without it – yet another one of those many minor miracles.

On or about 6 March, all the camp inmates who had been there when we arrived were moved to an adjacent camp before shortly afterwards vanishing altogether. Among their number was Fredy Hirsch. The word from the neighbouring camp was that he had taken an overdose the night before (the means to that end must have been supplied by his Nazi contacts, I imagine). We were told nothing officially, but the fact the inmates disappeared exactly six months after their arrival and that the chimneys were spouting smoke conveyed an ominous message. Yet I cannot remember worrying about the clear implication regarding my own future. Either I have forgotten something or, more likely, the business of day-to-day survival obscured any concerns about what was in store for us three months hence.

In May a new transport arrived from Terezín. Thereafter, there were intermittent arrivals from other parts of Europe. The Dutch and Hungarians, in particular, seemed to go to pieces very quickly. The weather turned hot, the mud dried up, and we were put to work carrying out pointless tasks – such as filling holes in the ground that others had just been made to dig.

I had another remarkable escape worth recording. The squad to which I had been assigned was ordered to carry bricks around the camp perimeter, which most of us did using our outstretched arms. That proved painful so I, naturally, carried the bricks on my back in a sling made out of my belt. Unfortunately the belt broke, causing the bricks to fall to the ground. The guard, who had been watching me, unleashed his Alsatian, which charged towards me. It came to me in a flash that, if I ran, the dog would bring me down and probably maul me, so I stood still and faced it down. The dog stopped and seemed uncertain what to do next; it had evidently not been programmed for such an eventuality. And then in yet another stroke of luck: not only did the dog's aggression evaporate, but so did the guard's. Perhaps he was shamed by his dog's lack of military resolve, but I was allowed to pick up my bricks in peace.

By mid June our six months were up, but there was a departure from the predestined plan. Starting around 7 July, the older teenagers, myself included, along with the fitter-looking men, were ordered to strip and parade past SS officers seated at a table. When interrogated, I added a year to my real age and, thanks in part to having had to carry heavy barrels and perhaps also to the sugar and chicory mixture, I graduated to slave labourer. After a few days in an adjacent camp, I found myself among a group being loaded into the backs of open lorries and driven off. That was the last time I saw my mother and brother.

At the time I could not fully understand the significance of what was going on around me, which was, perhaps, just as well. The entire transport that left in March had been liquidated in the gas chambers. That included Fredy Hirsch (it is still a matter of debate whether he was dead, unconscious or merely sedated at the time).

Years elapsed before I was able to integrate these events into a historical framework. Even outside the camps, the progress of the war was obscured throughout occupied Europe by the Nazi propaganda machine. Within the camps, rumours were rife but could not be given much credence. However, evidently Hitler's original plans based on continuing Nazi victories had come badly unstuck. German forces were being depleted in Russia and, in early June 1944, the D-Day landings made further demands on manpower. So by the time it was our turn to be gassed, Hitler was forced to decide that his need for slave labourers took precedence over any rapid implementation of the 'final solution'.

My brother was too young to work. I am convinced that, given the choice, my mother would have gone to the gas chambers with him but I doubt that was an option. I believe she died in some other slave labour camp. All my attempts to trace her, all my searches of archives for further information, have proved futile. It does not do to dwell on these thoughts if one wants to live the semblance of a normal life, but I invite anyone who wishes to share my nightmares to picture that group of children, including my terrified little brother, being herded into the gas chamber. He had such a short and miserable childhood; I often wish I could have been a more supportive brother to him.

It is worth noting that the mass gassing on 8 March, followed by the liquidation of the remainder of the family camp, 10–12 July 1944, constituted the biggest mass murder by far of Czechoslovak citizens during World War II.

I was now on my own, but at least had no one else to worry about.

7

Blechhammer

My departure from Auschwitz evoked a very different mood from that of my arrival there. Now I was in the back of an open lorry, in midsummer, not locked in a cattle truck on a dark December night, and my spirits lifted on seeing green grass and trees again. The Birkenau Familienlager had been a desolate wasteland of mud and barbed wire, shunned by nature – as seemed appropriate for that purpose-built holding pen for the gas chambers. Although I was unknowingly heading towards much greater physical suffering, nothing in my later recollections matches the horror of that blackest hole of pure evil, whose sole purpose was genocide on an industrial scale.

I had no idea how long I was travelling for or, indeed, where I was – beyond that it must be somewhere in Polish Silesia. My movements remained a mystery to me for most of my life. Even had I not tried so successfully to put that entire period out of my mind, concentration camps were not marked on any German maps accessible to the public and it would have been hard indeed to locate my position using only a few remembered landmarks and my intuition. It was not until I reached the age of eighty-two and had been persuaded to write down my experiences that I tried to retrace my movements. By then, the world had changed and it took me just a few minutes to Google the shortest route from Auschwitz to Blechhammer, which is just under a hundred kilometres via Katowice and Gliwice.

Never having been back, I find satellite images of the camps particularly disturbing; I was shocked to recognize my barrack in Birkenau, now surrounded by lawns and trees. Somehow turning it into parkland seems offensive to me and all wrong – it would have been right to have kept the soil covered in bleaching powder so that nothing would ever grow there again.

Looking out the back of the lorry, it cheered me to see small villages and ordinary people; people who were neither prisoners, guards, nor soldiers. I expect this will seem weird to anyone who has not thought about the effect on a teenager's psyche of eighteen months' incarceration, without any expectation of ever again seeing even such very restricted glimpses of normality. Besides, my spirits rose at the thought that whatever it was I had been selected for, it was not an imminent passive death.

Blechhammer appears to have been built as a labour camp before it became a concentration camp, part of the cluster of slave labour establishments administered by Auschwitz. It was located in a rather beautiful forested area and became a dormitory camp for slave labourers who serviced a huge industrial complex. The main purpose of the central facility was the operation of a plant for converting pulverised coal to petroleum products by some variant of the Fischer–Tropsch process. Early every morning, prisoners were marched in long columns, escorted by Wehrmacht soldiers, to various parts of the facility, returning to the camp late at night.

When we first arrived, we had the full sauna treatment: our heads were shaved and we were disinfested, showered, and kitted out with blue shirt, underpants, striped pyjamas, cap, and clogs with canvas tops. As luck would have it, my first issue fitted reasonably well, though, as the process was regularly repeated, that was by no means the usual state of affairs and we were often driven to some clandestine swapping when the opportunity presented itself. On the plus side, the showers dispensed only water; there was a crematorium at Blechhammer but no gas chambers. However, being too ill to work was a one-way ticket to the Auschwitz gas chambers.

We – the first group of Czech teenagers, newly arrived from Auschwitz-Birkenau – were assigned to the construction and maintenance of the works' rail-tracks. We acted in a manner which, in retrospect, seems very stupid. Instead of trying to sabotage the operation, we decided to act as an elite workforce. We marched out each morning whistling merrily, trying to look fitter than our military escort. (That was not difficult; the Wehrmacht types who were supposed to guard us were a far cry from the Auschwitz SS thugs – they were decrepit elderly soldiers shambling under the weight of their basic rifles, clearly unfit to serve the Fatherland in active service at the front in any of the many theatres of war.) I shall explain why we acted in this way, but let it be said at once that it resulted in the understandable loathing of the old hands; mostly Polish Jews who had arrived in Blechhammer long before us.

The nature of the work changed completely once the air raids started. Before that, our task was to carve a smooth straight bed out of the forest soil using spades and shovels, and then lay a deep stone substrate for the wooden sleepers, using a kind of broad short-handled gardening fork with rounded ends to the tines. I could barely lift it when it was fully laden with stones. There were other strange and wonderful implements. After the sleepers had been put into place, rails were carried in huge tongues, at least one man to each handle. This involved the entire team working in two rows with the rail in between (unless one had the good fortune to be the odd man out). Finally, the stones were compacted under the sleepers using a kind of pick-axe, one end of which had a blunt hammer instead of the spike. I dare say that all these, to me outlandish, tools were used on rail-tracks everywhere at that time.

Our instructors and supervisors were two young Polish civilians, presumably employees of the railway company. For all their huffing and puffing they were decent people, to which the following story bears witness. Their German overseer was an avid hunter and the Silesian forests all around offered plenty of game. Marksmanship was evidently not his strongest suit because, some weeks after our arrival on the scene, he managed to shoot and kill his own hunting dog – a large Alsatian. In an uncharacteristically generous act, the officer donated the canine carcass to our Polish supervisors, who cooked a splendid meal from its mortal remains. (They were also short of food, of course; protein in particular.) We did not get any of the meat – that would have been too much to hope for – but we got some of the soup. I have never forgotten either that act of kindness or the delicious taste of the soup. I dare say that not many people have tasted Alsatian soup, but it was the best meal I had that year.

All the members of our teenage gang suffered from extreme sleep deprivation. As a physical craving, it came only just second to hunger. I had no watch, of course, or sight of a clock to refer to, but I doubt we ever got more than four hours' sleep. Our days started before dawn with the early-morning roll call. This required us to stand to attention in rows and columns of multiples of ten to be counted. The only valid excuse for not attending was having died during the night; any other dereliction would lead to grotesque punishments. We were often kept standing for hours when the task was assigned to an officer who would find even counting out loud so taxing that he would repeatedly lose track and have to start again. The SS officers who had problems counting on their fingers, spoke atrocious, strongly accented German; they may have been Polish *Volksdeutsche* volunteers. During the long days of the summer we would sway with tiredness during repeated miscounts but when winter came, and we had to stand for hours in the freezing cold in our thin prison pyjamas, we suffered from serious hypothermia – to the very point of passing out. The procedure was repeated after our return in the evening. ('To stand up and be counted' has sinister implications for me to this day.)

The sleep deprivation accounts for our 'elite workforce' act. It was an attempt to bribe our supervisors into allowing us brief naps, on the grounds that our exceptional effort would make them look good in the eyes of their German overseers. We would bargain to complete a massive length of track within a certain time in return for a rest period when it was completed. It was an ill-conceived idea, doomed to failure. All I can say in our defence is that our supervisors were also too stupid to see the risk, at least to begin with. They were cunning enough to try and cheat us by setting ever-higher targets, but they did not consider the consequences of the German overseer turning up unexpectedly to find us snoozing on a pile of wooden sleepers. There was hell to pay, of course. Thereafter we learned what the old hands had been doing all along – napping while leaning on our shovels whenever nobody was watching – and our productivity approached the norm.

One would imagine that such utter exhaustion would at least result in deep dreamless sleep at night, but no. A nightly torture of the camps and one of my worst torments was to wake from dreams of happy episodes from my childhood to the nightmare of where I now found myself.

One reason for the nightly frequent interruptions was the fact that most of our diet, such as it was, consisted mostly of soup, with the obvious physiological consequence of being in need of frequent urination. Unfortunately, the latrines were a good 300 metres from my barrack. Although the path was in full sight of the nearest watchtower, after a while I decided I might perhaps urinate on the hoof without getting shot. This is a skill that has to be learned, but, after a week or so, I found that my need for the latrine disappeared after I covered about a third of the distance. I have often wondered what the guards made of my changes of mind and reversals of direction. In winter, of course, this performance played itself out in deep snow and I created pretty Jackson Pollock–type yellow tracings on a snow-white background, all in the glare of the watchtowers' searchlights. As I did not get shot, I like to think the guards welcomed the nightly diversion I provided during their long, cold night watches. Back in my hut I had to climb up to my level of the bunk, of course, and shoehorn my cold, occasionally moist, person among the tightly packed bodies of my sleeping partners. Since we all had similar needs, our predicament was hardly conducive to even a short night's deep sleep.

One aspect of Blechhammer that made our lives easier to bear was that here we had some contact with the outside world. This was purely visual, of course; we were not allowed to interact with civilians, but even seeing ordinary people going about their work was a treat after one and a half years in the camps. Also, I was occasionally able to scan scraps of discarded German newspapers on the ground, which helped me feel part of the human race, even though the news was always depressing. There were no German losses, according to the papers, only victories. In particular, I read about the newly developed

V weapons, which were about to destroy England (including my father) for good. No one could have guessed from what I glimpsed that we were within a year of the total defeat of the Third Reich.

And then came the air raids. The Germans must have anticipated this development. They had lost access to some of the oilfields in the East and the production of synthetic oil became an imperative. In addition to sirens and anti-aircraft gun emplacements, they had been building massive air raid shelters. I saw one of them in the process of construction at the time we arrived. Workmen were pouring concrete over an iron framework encased in a wooden shell, which had evidently been designed for multiple uses. The shelter was a long semicylindrical tunnel, terminating in square towers with entrances at right angles; the walls must have been six feet thick. Much later I saw the effect of a direct hit by a bomb on one such tunnel. It took a chunk out of the concrete that was but a small proportion of the wall's thickness. I was told that two people inside were killed, either by the shockwave that traversed the wall against which they were leaning, or due to some equipment that had been fixed to the wall falling on them. There is no doubt, however, that most of those inside would have survived any number of direct hits. All this was of academic interest to us, since we were not allowed into shelters.

There were also thick-walled metal drums disposed at frequent intervals all along the plant's roads. They were fitted with showerheads which generated a thick fog to obscure the works by discharging liquid chemicals (titanium tetrachloride?) which reacted with the moisture in the atmosphere. The fog felt painfully corrosive to the lungs, particularly when deeply inhaled in large gulps by someone fleeing from the bombing and out of breath. Cloaking the works turned out to be rather pointless, since the USAF engaged in high-altitude carpet-bombing. Indeed, on one glorious occasion, when a steady wind moved the entire cloud of chemical smokescreen over the forest, they bombed the forest instead.

The bombing started one sunny day when we were distracted from our work by two twin-engine planes flying very fast at low altitude, below the tops of the factory chimneys. It only occurred to me much later that they were carrying out photographic reconnaissance. (Actually my dominant feeling, whenever I saw Allied planes, was envy of the lucky pilots who, incredibly, would be back in their own beds, in the free world, just a few hours later.) In the following days, workmen were shortening the factory chimneys so they would not protrude through the chemical fog.

After that, the bombers arrived every sunny Friday. Many years later I learned that the capture of airbases in northern Italy had just brought Blechhammer within the range of the new USAF Flying Fortress bombers. I saw them on one occasion when I got caught in the open, not having managed to find shelter between the howling of sirens and the drone of the aircraft. They were flying in formation at, what seemed to me, an enormous height, like a white high-altitude cloud. (At that time I had never seen aircraft at such a height; nowadays one cannot look at the sky without seeing several airliners at that altitude.) They carpet-bombed the works without, as far as I could judge, breaking formation or changing altitude. On that occasion a bomb exploded so close to me that, lying on the ground, I felt my legs flailing through the air. Fortunately I was not hurt, except for damage to my hearing which persists to this day. Because of the soft forest soil, the bombs penetrated deeply before exploding, producing steep sided, narrow craters.

One tried, of course, not to get caught in the open. Our guards bolted into official air raid shelters, from which we were barred, at the first note of the sirens. We were left to look for whatever nearby bolt-holes we could find, depending on where we were at the time. When we were close to the factory buildings, the object was to find the deepest cellar with the most floors above it.

On several occasions we ended up in a cellar storing coal dust under a very large building. That must have been either the central power station or the coal-to-petroleum conversion plant. What mattered was that it had some five stories above ground level. Not that we felt safe. The building got hit several times during each raid and we listened, in terror, to bombs penetrating floor by floor before exploding. We were rocked by powerful blast waves and listened to the debris falling before the next hit penetrated deeper. After the raid each of us emerged looking like a chimney sweeps' apprentice. Had I known then what I know now about coal dust explosions, I might have sought alternative shelter.

Sometimes we were working in areas where no suitable cover could be found. We then had to run and try to make it to the tunnels in the earth banks which surrounded the plant periphery. My father had taught me how to cover long distances as quickly as possible by alternating running with, when completely out of breath, fast walking (though we did not plan for the corrosive effects on lungs of large gulps of chemical fog). Not only were the earth banks far away, but they would offer only very limited protection. They would stop most of the bomb casing shrapnel but they would certainly not withstand a direct hit.

I had been led to believe that bombs whistle as they descend, but that was not at all what we experienced when carpet-bombed by large bomber formations. Instead there was a terrifying juddering vibration that shook the lungs and body, rising to an unbearable crescendo when the concussions were on top of us. My experiences in the camps generally have made me something of a connoisseur of what causes blind panic, and I have no hesitation in putting this particular experience right at the top of my list of terrors.

Curiously, until I started writing this, I had always associated that throbbing tremor with the interaction of a large number of bombs travelling through the atmosphere at great speed, perhaps approaching sonic terminal velocities. Having now seen film footage of carpet-bombing filmed from above which shows individual shock waves, I have come to realise that what we were hearing and feeling was the superimposition of successive waves of blast-fronts from the approaching leading edge of the bomb 'carpet', coming at us horizontally, not vertically. In terms of timing and duration the outcome would have been much the same; the altitude of the planes must have been of the same order as the dimensions of the plant and the terminal velocity of the bombs not that different from that of the approaching leading edge of the 'carpet' – that is, the speed of the planes.

As we were sitting there on piles of wooden planks in the crescendo of throbbing air, terrified by the gigantic forces that would imminently tear us to pieces, I saw everyone's eyes closed and lips moving in silent supplication. I knew that many of those praying professed not to be believers, but there were no atheists in that tunnel in the sand. I have been thinking about my friends' beliefs in the intervening years. What they had rejected, I think, is religion – yet when in mortal peril they craved the comfort afforded by prayer to a personal god. The concepts of organised religion and personal belief are quite distinct, in my view. It may be that the predisposition to believe in a personal god originates in childhood from our dependence on a dominant parental figure for comfort and protection. However, since belief in a god is such a powerful aid to survival, evolution over many generations must have resulted in a god-shaped space, or template, in our minds. That would explain why all human communities have worshipped a god or gods. Religions, on the other hand, are in my view clearly man-made and have just exploited these innate feelings. The calling of priest, druid, prophet, shaman – indeed whoever puts on a funny hat and says, 'God has spoken to me and has told me that I am his representative on Earth and the only path to his ultimate authority'- is probably the second oldest profession. The message varies in its detail but, in general, promises eternal suffering should you be inclined to ignore it, and, above all, it requires adherents to abhor and persecute the competition – that is, all other religions. Who can count the deaths, the dreadful suffering, that religious conflicts have unleashed on mankind, and continue to do so? My poor friends therefore had rejected religion. When in fear of their lives, they desperately sought to retrieve the baby they had thrown out with the bathwater – or so it seemed to me.

Anyhow, we survived on that occasion; others were not so lucky. One of the shelters, which was essentially just a cave in the ground surmounted by a large mound of soil, had been hit and collapsed, burying the occupants. By that time we had returned to our tools at the track we had been working on and were about to begin the rescue work. Unfortunately, an SS guard turned up to inspect the damage. We had our shovels on our shoulders, ready to dig out the poor devils in the collapsed shelter, but were ordered to return to the rail-track repairs. That was the occasion when we got closest to mutiny. The guard drew his pistol, yelling that he would kill anyone who disobeyed the order to return to work. We had, of course, never established any connection with our guards, but this was the first time I was actually staring down the muzzle of a gun. The

93

devastation and carnage of the air raids had brought us to the front line of the war.

There were fires, buildings reduced to rubble, craters in the roads, telegraph poles broken like matchsticks and power lines lying on the ground – some of them displaying bright sizzling arc discharges from severed strands of wire. There were also punctured fog canisters with acrid chemical smoke gushing through the shrapnel holes. What bombs did to our rails was quite spectacular, especially if they struck between them: they blasted them apart and turned the ends of the tracks into gigantic ladders.

The rail-tracks ran alongside roads and above them were massive pipes on gantries. Some of the pipes carried flammable liquids – at least they did while the plant was still operational. So what we were called upon to fix was often a broken track pointing to the skies, one rail of which had punctured an overhead pipe and had flaming oil running down it. The procedure, once the flames were extinguished, required the damaged track to be replaced. Unbolting the bent rail caused it to fall instantly and at great speed. The direction was unpredictable, as was that on rebound, after the twisted metal had hit the ground. We did our best to get out of the way, of course, but it was pure chance that none of us was killed.

Speaking of more miracles, some of the things that happened to me seem so implausible now that I have seriously considered leaving them out, lest the reader should suspect I made them up. On second thoughts, that would have been just as dishonest as fabrication, so here goes. Sometimes the anti-aircraft guns would open up after the warning sirens went off, but long before any aircraft appeared. I do not know what they were doing; perhaps they were calibrating the height at which the shells exploded. Every now and again we heard a patter as if large hailstones were falling all around us. They were pieces of flak shrapnel, with jagged edges and too hot to touch. On that occasion it occurred to me that it might perhaps be a good idea to hold my mess tin on top of my head. Presently, there was a loud bang, and a big dent appeared in the substantial metal container. In utter amazement, I offered up a silent prayer of thanks to my guardian angel.

By late autumn it must have been obvious to everybody that all the labouring by thousands of workers of every speciality was a total waste of time – a highly treasonable thought, since the entire German war machine depended critically on continued oil supplies. Had there been just a single, more specifically targeted air raid, the damage might perhaps have been repaired, in due course. But repeated carpet-bombing destroyed all the infrastructure, along with the main objectives, so that nothing worked. It was clear that the Germans would henceforth not produce enough petrol to fill their cigarette lighters.

The camp Kommandatur reacted, characteristically, by executing one of ours for sabotage. One evening when we had marched back to the camp, we were all lined up in squares, as for a roll call. It was obvious what was going to happen because what we had to face was a podium with one of the concrete posts, normally used as supports for the high-tension barbed wire fencing, erected on it and a chair placed underneath its arched top. The camp commandant, who had turned up with the prisoner, several helpers and rope, made a brief speech. I managed to blank out most of it but it specified the death penalty for sabotage.

I tried my usual device again of blanking my mind – looking without seeing or registering – but was disturbed by a gasp from the assembled crowd when the rope snapped and the man fell on the stage. Incredibly, the entire action was replayed for a second time, with the same result. Evidently, the helpers must have tampered with the ropes, on the assumption that no man can be hanged twice. They should have known that the Nazis would not recognize any such law; on the third attempt, with a new rope, the poor man died at last.

The act of 'sabotage' for which he was executed was one of which many of us were guilty. When I described our footwear earlier, I did not mention that the laces were made of a material little stronger than twisted paper. They tended to disintegrate, particularly when wet. One then hobbled until a suitable substitute lace was found. Fortunately, it generally did not take too long to find more or less suitable pieces of string or wire lying about the work place. After the air raids, a new and very effective source, in the form of thin insulated telephone wires became plentiful. Unfortunately, one end of the wire was generally still attached to a fallen telegraph pole. Since it was obvious that the system was beyond repair, it never even occurred to us that liberating a suitable length to use as a bootlace might be misrepresented as sabotage. The hanging brought about a rapid reappraisal of our substitute bootlace materials. The Germans could kill us at a whim anyhow; there seemed little merit in offering them additional inspiration.

Autumn turned to winter and the weather became very cold, with frost and snow. We suffered hypothermia during extended roll calls; this was used as a form of punishment. What we did not know about, though I suppose that the Germans must have suspected in spite of all their propaganda, was the rout of their armies on the Eastern front and hence the imminent threat from the Russians. In fact the onset of the Russian offensive marked the New Year of 1945 and by January 21 our evacuation from Blechhammer had started. Thereafter, we could occasionally hear the sound of heavy guns.

Not everybody left. A friend of mine hid in one of the many potato-clamps around the periphery of the camp. The Germans searched the barracks very thoroughly but only tossed hand grenades down the ventilation ducts of the clamps. Our guards seemed in a great hurry to leave, no doubt imagining what fate would befall them if the Russian army caught up with them herding columns of emaciated slave labourers in striped pyjamas. (Russian soldiers, particularly those who survived Nazi occupation, had a pretty gruesome reputation for executing summary justice.) My friend was not injured by the grenades and was liberated by Konev's army. I learned after the war, however, that, as the scion of an extremely rich manufacturer of railway locomotives, he was sent to a Soviet re-education camp.

I have often wondered how differently my subsequent life might have turned out had I tried to hide as he did. Looking at the outcome statistically, the chance of not being killed by the hand grenades was probably marginally better than that of surviving what happened to the rest of the prisoners. On the other hand, had I been liberated by the Soviets, I would probably not have been able to join my father in England before the Iron Curtain descended, but these are idle speculations.

We got a packed lunch for the march: an unusually large (but still less than a kilogram, I would guess) chunk of our usual 'sawdust bread', some margarine (which I suspect contained hydrogenated inorganic oil) and some of the artificial white lumpy mass euphemistically called 'honey'. It may be that nobody foresaw that the march would last twelve days.

So, having arrived in Blechhammer on a hot summer's day on the back of a lorry wearing my own clothes, I left seven months later, on foot, in freezing weather, trudging through deep snow on wood-soled feet wearing thin prison 'pyjamas'.

9

The Longest Walk,
the Coldest Train Journey

Once again I had no concept of where I was or where we were heading until I searched through the documentation now available on the web, sixty-four years down the line. It transpires, we walked via Kole – Neustadt – Glucholazy – Neisse – Otmuchow – Zabkowice Slaskie – Schweidnitz – Strzegom until we, the survivors, reached Gross-Rosen concentration camp, twelve days later. Many gave up and fell by the wayside, knowing that would end their lives. Everybody has a breaking point when, no matter how strong the spirit, the body and brain give up. Thanks to my youth and history, I had not quite reached that stage, but was not far off. I learned later that some 800 of us died or were killed en route. The bodies were piled high on horse-drawn farm carts which brought up the rear. We walked through forests, along roads, across fields, all covered in snow.

We may not have known where we were heading but it was perfectly clear what we were fleeing from. And we were not alone. We were being overtaken by smaller, faster parties of

POWs in smart air force and other allied military uniforms. They had fewer guards and actually had some personal possessions, which they pulled along on small sledges.

Every now and again we had a special treat: a fast-moving convoy of the retreating German army would force us into a ditch. When leaping into a ditch, one hoped fervently that it was frozen all the way to the bottom and did not contain liquid water or mud. But for us, the indignity and discomfort was well worth the spectacle of seeing the frozen, exhausted, dejected, ashen-faced soldiers, their limbs swathed in bloody bandages, of that beaten army as they swept past us on their gun chariots. In our situation, and remembering their former swagger and the atrocities they had perpetrated, it would have taken a heart of stone not to be filled with joy at the sight. Appropriately, our feelings could be described by the German word 'Schadenfreude'. Maybe we were witnessing the dawning of some justice, unlikely though we were to see it come to fruition. There is a famous nineteenth-century painting by Adolf Northern entitled *Napoleon's Retreat from Moscow*. Different uniforms and no motorized transport, of course, but the facial expressions of dejected, humbled arrogance are identical. It should act as a dire warning to any little man with overweening ambitions not to presume to take on the Russian winter.

Our progress was called a march but, truly, it was more of a trudge, a shuffle, a limp. At night we were locked in farm outbuildings, barns and sheds. On one occasion I bedded down on what looked like a comfortable pile of white powder, only to wake shortly afterwards to a burning sensation along my back; I must have chosen a heap of some chemical fertilizer for my bed. More often it was straw.

Occasionally it was possible to find something to eat. Bits of turnips, swedes, even rotten cabbage leaves all yielded some small amount of nourishment. I conceived the impression that one could not quite starve in farming country. I do not recollect having to defecate during the entire period of the march. The one highly calorific food I was unable to eat was sugar beet. One mouthful was all I could manage before the overpowering sweetness turned to bitterness and nausea.

One night I noticed a cow in a stall next to our barn and sneaked out in the middle of the night, intending to milk it into the lid of my mess tin. I had never milked a cow before but had often seen it done. The cow seemed content – or at least it did not kick me in the face, as I had feared – as I squeezed with my fingers in a downward sequence. I managed to extract a few squirts, before the tread of a guard's boots on the snow caused me to flee. Still, I got one or two mouthfuls of nourishing warm milk.

When we slept on deep straw, some people tried to hide by burrowing deep into it before the next morning's departure. When the guards came to collect us, they fixed bayonets to their guns and pierced the straw in many places. I would never take such a risk, chiefly because, if truth be told, I have always been more concerned about the manner than the time of my death. Ideally, I would like to meditate on all the wonderful experiences of my life, fall asleep, and not wake up. Freezing to death often seemed an attractive option because, once one became habituated to the agony of the biting cold, forcing oneself to stay alive felt rather like fighting fatigue and an over-powering desire to lie down and go to sleep. During the total exhaustion and cold of the march, the soft white snow looked most inviting. Being stabbed with a bayonet, on the other hand, would be the extreme antithesis of what I had in mind for my passing. (As an aside, it seems a sad reflection on today's values that any public demand for the legal freedom to choose the manner of one's death prompts an instant chorus of axe-grinding by a lobby of religious zealots and professors of palliative medicine.)

Some unlikely items, such as old newspapers and string, became valuable commodities. Newspapers provide good light-weight insulation from the cold; string is needed to hold them in place. Initially I had an old pair of knitted socks, god knows from where. When the feet of the socks finally disintegrated completely, I stuffed any old paper I could find in their place.

I developed frostbite on both feet. It started where the folds in the footwear uppers pressed on the top of the foot, just behind the big toe joints (where I bear the scars to this day). What happens with frostbite, if nothing is done about it, is that the tissue dies and stops hurting. Gradually more of the toes are affected and the damage spreads. Of those few of us who survived, a substantial proportion had to have their toes ampu-tated. It did not happen to me because I swapped my boots for those of others who had no further use for them; there were plenty of corpses in the barns every morning. All the boots pinched and hurt, of course, but not in quite the same place, which was the point.

Usually I had to try on more than one pair in what little time there was. My window of opportunity increased over the days as our escorts, especially the old Wehrmacht types, became quite sluggish in the mornings. They had better clothing and, presumably, some food, but at least we did not have to carry heavy guns or be on night guard duty.

So, on the twelfth day, what was left of our columns limped – just dragging one foot in front of the other, on automatic – into the Gross-Rosen concentration camp.

I do not remember much of my stay in Gross-Rosen beyond one or two flashbacks. One I mentioned previously is of blackened corpses hanging on the high-tension barbed wire fences. In Gross-Rosen it was evidently possible to commit suicide by electrocution in that way without being shot, at least at that time. What with hundreds arriving on foot and being dispatched by rail, it was a totally chaotic situation. On examining historical archives, I was surprised to learn that my stay there must have lasted five days; I would have thought two or three, but perhaps it depends on whether the days of arrival and departure are included in the count.

I do not believe that, on this occasion, my amnesia arose from the deliberate suppression of memory. The truth is that by that time I was so exhausted, emaciated and frozen that my brain no longer functioned normally. I was only half alive. Perhaps under such conditions death is not a discontinuity but a more gradual process. One hoped that the state might be reversible – though, as in the case of frozen toes, there is no way of reviving parts that have passed a point of no return.

Long after these events, I wondered why it was necessary to drag us to Gross-Rosen for transport to Buchenwald. When the tide of the war turned, Hitler decreed that no live prisoner be allowed to fall into Allied hands. The murderous Einsatzgruppen were charged with ensuring that outcome. I assume that the Russian push in the North was so rapid that trying to use the Auschwitz railhead would have incurred the risk of being overrun before evacuation was complete and Gross-Rosen was the closest suitable railhead still considered safe at the time. In fact, the Russians liberated Gross-Rosen on 13 February, just about a week after our departure. I have that information from a Gross-Rosen inmate who had the job of burying the corpses brought in by the wooden carts that followed the marchers. After liberation by the Russians, he had another long trek home to Czechoslovakia.

I like to think that the progressive adjustments in Hitler's 'solution' to his rhetorical 'Jewish question' afford some insight into the state of his mind. The intended final outcome never changed, of course, but the process of getting there seemed to pass through three phases. While his Blitzkrieg was overrunning Western Europe and the Third Reich was destined 'to last a thousand years', the only technical problem was disposing of the vast number of corpses, killing being so much quicker and easier than cremation or burial. By the time I was sent to Blechhammer, however, he needed to keep slave labourers alive a little longer, as the war had totally depleted German manpower. In the third phase, did the decree that no live prisoner be allowed to fall into Allied hands presage a fear that there might dawn a day of reckoning and justice, when anyone left alive could act as witnesses to his atrocities?

The train we were herded onto was made up of open rail trucks of the kind used to transport coal. The side panels were only about a metre high. It was late afternoon and almost dark. Experience had taught me to head straight for a side wall so I would have something to lean against, to support my back. I was lucky to find such a space quite near a corner, opposite where we climbed in. I emphasise my luck because it soon became apparent that there were too many of us, at least in our wagon, for everyone to find adequate seating space. We might perhaps have done better had there been more light and some organisation amongst us. There was instead much shoving and pushing as people realised that being thrown about on a long journey would weigh the odds heavily against survival. Once seated, it was impossible to move – any gap opened up would instantly vanish under other bony bottoms.

In the tumult, a very large Pole who could not find a space decided to sit on top of me; I suppose that I looked small and vulnerable. Had he succeeded that would have been the end of me since he was twice my size. I was saved by another small miracle. When I put my arms behind my back to brace myself, my hand felt a small metallic object, which turned out to be a tiny pair of ladies' nail scissors. The truck had evidently been used to transport people before.

I could not actually bring myself to stab another human being – not now, not then. Let us say that I permitted his posterior to make first contact with the pointed end of the nail scissors held on my knees, when he slumped on top of me. There was much Polish swearing and the flailing of big fists, but it was too dark by then and too crowded for him to pinpoint the culprit. (Incidentally, much as I love the richness of the English language, when it comes to swearing, it is not in the same league as the Slav idiom in terms of profundity, depth and inventiveness.)

Although I did not cause serious hurt, the episode helps to explain why I am thankful, but never proud, to have survived the camps. In my view, we, the survivors, are all somewhat compromised. We did not sacrifice our lives so that others might perhaps stand a slightly better chance of living. As it is, survival feels less like a heroic act than like having won a lottery against truly astronomical odds. It is easy to fantasise that there must have been some profound underlying reason for one's survival, but in the end it was probably just a combination of chance and an aptitude for self-preservation.

As far as I can make out, the distance between Gross-Rosen and Buchenwald (near Weimar) is about 400 kilometers. A very slow train should cover it in around eight hours. Our journey lasted three or four days (according to the archives; my recollection is of countless nights and days). Our train spent most of that time being shunted into sidings to make way for troop and other more important war transport. We witnessed several air raids and came to believe that we had simply been forgotten and would die there (as many of us indeed did). We were not given anything to eat or drink. Fortunately we had plenty of snow. Not very nourishing but at least we did not become completely dehydrated. Snow was a mixed blessing but, had it been raining, we would not have had the means to accumulate water to drink in useful quantities.

On one occasion an Allied fighter pilot strafed us, presumably having mistaken the train for a troop transport, in spite of our striped pyjamas. Fortunately our truck was not hit. It made me appreciate the truth of the saying that there is always somebody worse off. Being squashed between bodies, some of which were clearly already dead and literally frozen stiff, was bad enough but at least it was quiet and peaceful. It does not bear thinking about what it would have been like to be unable to help people who were wounded and wailing in pain, to have to sit in congealing freezing blood for days on end.

When we arrived, on 10 February 1945, I was one of the few who were able to dismount from the truck unaided. There were many frozen corpses. I do not know how many died; I did not stop to count. I must have been on autopilot, not even realising that I was within an hour of total collapse. If I was half dead in

Gross-Rosen, it must have been more like three quarters now. It is difficult to explain the feeling to someone who has not experienced it, but one's perception is dimmed, one is on automatic, there is a feeling of impending total oblivion.

9

Buchenwald

In my wildest dreams I could not have imagined that a concentration camp 'sauna' would feel like paradise. After the usual dusting with DDT (or the German equivalent of delousing powder) there were showers. They were warm; the hall was warm. I had forgotten warm. It was bliss. I had not felt warm since the autumn frosts started almost half a year earlier.

I decided to give up the fight here. This was a good place to die, I thought. I was not going out in the cold again, ever. I lay on the floor and was not going to get up; I believe that I passed out.

Had my brain been functioning normally, I would have guessed that dying in the drying room of the sauna would be against the rules. I came to regret my moment of weakness soon afterwards. When I came round, I was on a stretcher being carried through the snow by two seasoned Buchenwald inmates. Based on my Auschwitz experience, I assumed that we were heading for the gas chambers. My worst fears were corroborated when, in response to my feeble protestations, in Czech, one of the men laughed rather callously and said, also in Czech: 'You should have thought of that earlier.'

However, although so many perished there, Buchenwald was not designated as an extermination camp and there were no gas chambers. I was taken to the *Krankenbau*. To translate that as 'hospital' would be a travesty. Patients were lying tightly packed into the usual four-storey bunks, making cross-infection inevitable. The only noticeable structural difference from dormitory barracks was an operating table in the centre and the only regular use of it I witnessed was the amputation of frozen toes from morning to night. The reason why my stretcher bearers assumed that they would not see me alive again was not gas, but the endemic typhus and dysentery, which spared no one. The Krankenbau was generally the end of the road.

After what I had just been through, however, I actually appreciated lying down indoors for a while. There was little comfort in the thin straw (or shredded paper, more likely) pallet under an even more inadequate blanket, but at least it afforded the opportunity to pass away under cover and in a recumbent attitude. I started near the entrance in the 'clean' section – 'clean' meaning before one showed symptoms of having contracted diarrhoea. The way the system worked was that so long as you could extricate yourself from your bunk and reach the latrine before you soiled yourself or your bedding, you could stay put. The latrine, however, seemed further and further away as time progressed. Remembering being ill in Ústí nad Orlicí after what I believe to have been a paratyphoid shot, I was hopeful that perhaps I had some immunity from the worst. It did not save me from dysentery however. After a few days, I was transferred, packaged in my bedding, to a recently vacated space in the 'dirty' section that was conveniently closer to the latrine, which I frequented at short intervals.

By way of diversion, my new abode had a grandstand view of the operating table, being located immediately above it. All day long an uninterrupted succession of frozen toes were snipped off and dropped into a bucket. This was followed by a dusting of Bolus Alba powder, with which I had become acquainted in Terezín, and bandaging. The bandages were not made of gauze fabric but looked more like a cross between crêpe and toilet paper. The procedure was probably not painful because the tissue was dead. (A friend of mine, a survivor of a different set of camps who lost all his toes, writes that he only noticed that several of them were missing when his boots were removed along with some of the toes left in them). I assume that the operation was essential if gangrene was to be avoided.

The surgeon had long white hair and a stick. He treated his patients like cattle. My guess was that he was an old political prisoner, probably a German Communist or homosexual, and that his victims were Polish Jews transported from the Silesian camps under conditions similar to those in my narrative. What was clear to me was his total lack of empathy; the surgeon did not respect, or care for, his 'patients'.

Eventually I was spending so much time on the latrine that it hardly seemed worth returning to my bunk and I was passing blood. I doubt anyone ever got out of there alive; it was a sort of assembly-line system for producing corpses. We would get weaker and weaker and when we died would be bundled up in our blood- and excreta-soaked pallets and incinerated in them, making way for the next batch. I felt very close to being next, in full view of the end of the conveyor belt.

And then, with the balance of probabilities tilted towards the almost-certain death region, there occurred the ultimate and utterly unexpected miracle which shifted the pointer back into the survival zone. An unknown man appeared in the doorway and called out loudly, in Czech: 'Are there any Czech boys in here?' The Czech stretcher bearer who brought me there on my first day in Buchenwald, which now seemed a long time ago, must have talked about me. I had thought him callous when he laughed at my plight but, as it turned out, he was instrumental in saving my life. I wasted no time in letting it be known loudly that there was indeed a Czech boy stuck in the dirty section.

So I was carried out of there and deposited into the charge of the Czech Communist Kapo (or *Block Aelteste*) Antonín Kalina. Communist barracks were run with ruthless discipline by the inmates themselves and here they accorded great respect to Kalina. He was a radical Communist but first and foremost a profoundly decent human being. I learned subsequently that he saved many other Jewish boys who had been transported from the Silesian camps and I am not at all convinced he had the enthusiastic support of the other political prisoners in this endeavour.

I met him only after industrial quantities of the all-purpose Bolus Alba put me back on my feet. Antonín Kalina had a lean, prematurely lined, much lived-in face. Having clearly marked me down as the son and heir of a capitalist family, he decided I was nevertheless not beyond redemption. The one thing we had in common, of course, is that we were both patriotic Czechs. He asked me whether we had servants at home, which I thought quite inappropriate, because I had actually always thought of Marie and Co. as friends and family. He asked me — somewhat contemptuously I thought — 'And what can you do?' So I told him I could sew on buttons, was generally handy with a needle and thread and particularly good at darning socks. That was no exaggeration. Following my early training in primary school, I used some of all that free time I had in Ústí nad Orlicí to darn all the extended families' socks. It was a task I enjoyed.

It was less honest to claim that I would be ideal at keeping his quarters tidy, since I must be one of the untidiest people in the world. However, I was enlisted on the spot and so became the batman of the Czech Communist Kapo, to the relief, I believe, of both of us, since he must have been wondering what to do with me. It gave me an indoor occupation and also explains why, to my surprise, I now appear in the Buchenwald archives as a political prisoner: Czech Communist.

Buchenwald was liberated on 11 April 1945 by the Sixth Armored Division of Patton's Third Army. Somewhere along the way the army, very fortunately, intercepted and eliminated the Einsatzgruppen heading our way. Ex-Buchenwald inmates may tell you that we in fact, liberated ourselves and, indeed, had secured the perimeter by the time the Americans took charge. Since, however, we did not storm the guard towers much earlier, our resolve may not have been unrelated to the imminent arrival of American tanks on our doorstep. Liberating ourselves and hanging at least one of the SS guards was a matter of pride, particularly to the Communist prisoners, who seemed to have managed to secrete some weaponry for the occasion. Personally, I took no active part and would have been perfectly happy to leave it to the Yanks since, unlike us, they were sitting inside tanks, which seemed a more fitting starting point.

There were the odd Nazi hardliners who decided to stay and fight and I suppose that the Americans, had we waited for them, might have opposed summary executions by the Communist prisoners. However, the GIs were so appalled by what they saw in the camp that they were willing to look the other way; I know of at least one such case. The majority of the Nazi guards, however, suddenly remembered urgent appointments else-where, as distant from the camp as possible, as the American armies approached. So urgent, in fact, was their departure they left their uniforms and weapons in the barracks for us to play with. In the event, most of them did not get beyond the nearby woods where they were soon rounded up by the Americans GIs, most of whom, to my particular delight, were black.

So, nine days after my seventeeth birthday, my life was given back to me. That took a long, long time to sink in. I am not sure it ever has entirely. Come to think of it, the concept is meaningless, since I was no longer the same person. The camps changed me permanently. While day-to-day survival had been my main concern, I had not done much thinking, so liberation called for a reappraisal of my life. It forced upon my attention the fact that I had just survived a crash course in the extreme suffering inflicted by attachments – be it to loved ones, cherished places or treasured possessions. Better try never to risk exposing myself in that way again.

It was years later that I learned that one Siddhartha Gautama came to much the same way of thinking some 2,500 years earlier, just by sitting under trees. Non-attachment proved easier while I was emotionally dead, during the first few years of my subsequent life. In the longer run, however, I found that the vulnerability that comes with attachments is forgotten in the happiness it brings.

This is not the end of the Buchenwald story. In fact I stayed there as long after liberation as before. The end of the war in Europe was still almost a month away. Bearing in mind the improbability of finding anyone I knew still alive at home, I was in no hurry to go back. I had an unrealistic hope that I might find some way of joining my father in England without having to return to Czechoslovakia first.

People kept on dying, many for the most stupid of reasons. Instinct told me that gorging on large helpings of pork stew (courtesy of the genius who liberated a pig from a nearby farm) was probably not the most intelligent way of ending three years of starvation. I must admit, though, that my instinct failed to predict that celebrating liberation by sunbathing on the roof of my barrack would lead to severe sunburn, due to my falling into an exhausted sleep, but that was far from lethal. The attraction of having a whole arsenal of German weapons to play with proved considerably more dangerous.

Some small arms came to light when I rummaged through the hastily vacated German barracks, a most exciting pastime. Anything might turn up: a dead guard – or perhaps a live one hiding in a wardrobe, waiting to swap uniforms with me. In my first foray, I managed to liberate a fine pair of Zeiss binoculars ('liberate' as in 'Hitler liberated the Sudeten from the Czechs') a sheepskin-lined leather jacket, which, after many years' service as my motorcycle undercoat, now rests in the Imperial War Museum's Holocaust exhibition and a Very signalling pistol with a great variety of different flare cartridges. The pistol was of about 1" calibre and had a kick like a mule. I abstained from picking up any lethal weapons but a pistol for DIY fireworks seemed a great toy. I avoided red flares, after I noticed that they seemed to induce some tumult in American tank movements, but my all-time favourites were magnesium flares which drifted down slowly on small parachutes. They turned night into day and, when the show was over, yielded a silken handkerchief when the parachute was detached. I could not remember when I had last owned a handkerchief, before these gifts from heaven.

I did nothing to advertise my trips but others inevitably followed, once they realized the potential for exploration and gain. On my second excursion I met a Czech boy who reminded me a little of my late friend Kurt. Not that he was unkempt, but he was tall and had a tendency to discuss philosophical topics with me. In those euphoric post-liberation days, friends were made quickly and easily. I don't remember seeing him before and do not think that he came via Blechhammer. I demonstrated my flare pistol to him and encouraged him to find one of his own.

Much later, I went back to the guards' quarters to look for him. I called to him but there was silence. What I found was a broad trail of blood on the floor, leading to the next room. There was my friend, dead on the floor, with his entrails hanging out of his abdomen, in a huge pool of blood. His head and hands were on a chair on which lay the pistol. He had evidently been trying to pull himself up on the chair in his final effort. To this day I do not know what happened. Perhaps some of the cartridges were small grenades, perhaps he forgot about the safety catch and stumbled; no one will ever know. One more corpse at that time would hardly have been noticed. I fled the room, deeply traumatised. It is another episode I have never fully recovered from. It may have been because of the jolt of total surprise and shock when I expected to talk to him; perhaps there was also some feeling of guilt associated with what happened. I had seen every conceivable horror, heaven knows, but this unexpected blow gave me my only direct experience of post-traumatic stress syndrome. It was the end of my foraging trips. For quite some time after the event I had a problem about entering an empty room on my own. My improvised snap-out-of-it-and-don't-be-so-silly brand of therapy helped me overcome the disorder but it took time.

The mass of the heavier German weaponry ended up in an enormous pile at the entrance of a quarry below the camp. It was bound to cause problems. Everything from heavy machine guns to hand grenades was there for the taking. And now there were also boys around who were much younger than the Blechhammer teenagers who arrived on my train. I am not sure where they came from, as they were too young to have been in labour camps or to have survived Auschwitz. Perhaps they had been evacuated from Terezín in the last few days. They enjoyed throwing hand grenades and waving guns about. There were accidents.

Eventually the Americans stepped in and ordered all weapons to be handed in. They then proceeded to deal with the matter in the most idiotic manner imaginable. All the weapons were piled up in a gigantic heap in a quarry below the camp. By that time I had moved to more comfortable quarters. My room actually had a window, which overlooked the quarry below and beyond, so I had a front-row view of the proceedings.

Some profound thinker had decided that the weapons would best be disposed of simply by blowing them up – confirming the adage that military intelligence is a contradiction in terms. So we were all ordered to stay indoors and close all windows and doors at the appointed hour. The explosive charge must have been huge. There was an enormous bang and shock wave, and the whole pile flew high up into the air and then fell back down, slightly rearranged. If the arms were dangerous before, they were lethal now. In the following days, I saw the most gruesome scenes from my window through my recently acquired binoculars. There was a type of small hand grenade shaped like a large tea egg. At its top was a colour-coded butterfly nut. As long as the colours did not match, it was safe to handle – or had been, before the explosion. I saw a boy pick one up, preparatory to throwing it. As he raised his arm, there was a flash and a bang and I saw the bloody wedge where his hand and wrist used to be, before he fell. I do not know what happened to him, but such terrible, senseless waste distressed me.

I too was attracted to the pile, though I was rather more circumspect about touching anything. My particular interest at the time was the *Panzerfaust* (armour fist), which was a new German shoulder-launched anti-tank weapon for use by a single individual. It looked rather like a modern RPG except that the anti-tank grenade was much larger. I wondered whether it was rocket-propelled or whether it was fired by a charge in the tube to which it was normally attached and which would then be left behind. Finding one of the tubes without its grenade, I thought there could be no great danger in pulling the trigger while the weapon was still on the ground (after the mishaps I had witnessed, I was not going to pick anything up). Well, there was a bang, the tube shot backwards and I felt something like a whiplash across the backs of my thighs (I was wearing shorts at the time). The backs of my legs were oozing blood but I could find no cut. It transpired that I was bleeding from lots of tiny puncture wounds; I believe that I still carry blast-sterilised grains of Buchenwald sand in my legs

Before very long, the Wild West interregnum, when there was no civil authority, came to an end. The Allied Expeditionary Forces Military Government and the Red Cross set up offices in Buchenwald. The former issued me with a provisional identity card (now also in the Imperial War Museum) certifying that I had been 'found' in KZ Buchenwald. At that instant I ceased to be, provisionally but officially, prisoner number 30529. From now on, if I died, I would no longer become a nameless collection of bones in a mass grave.

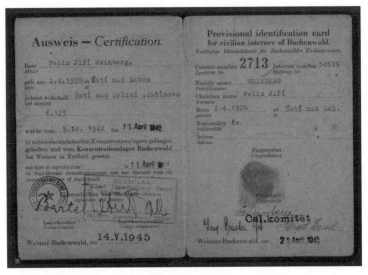

Provisional identity card certifying that I had been 'found' in KZ Buchenwald.

TELEPHONE
AVENUE 3266.

ADELAIDE HOUSE
LONDON BRIDGE
LONDON · E·C·4

14th May, 1945.

Dear Mr. Weinberg,

          I have just heard from
Dr.Kind to-day that your son has been
found at Buchenwald and I would like
to tell you how delighted I am at this
news. I sincerely hope that he has
not suffered too badly and that you will
soon be re-united with him.

          Let us hope that you
will soon hear from the rest of your
family.

          With kind regards,

          Yours sincerely,

          G. Tugendhat.

M/

The letter to my father informing him of my survival.

My father's last postal address, in Worsley, near Manchester, had been drilled into my memory by my mother and I made it clear to any of the officials who would listen that I wished to join my father in England as soon as possible. I had no reason to return to Czechoslovakia first. I believe the Red Cross managed to establish contact with my father and inform him of my survival. He clearly also received this information through other sources in due course.

I was befriended by a Col. Winter, an extremely kind US liaison officer. He made me a present of a US Commando Bowie knife, which is still a treasured possession of mine. It is very heavy and handy for lopping branches off trees. He often took me for outings in his jeep. In one of the first we passed a field near Weimar (the nearest town) where our former guards were held in a barbed wire enclosure. The weather on the day was dreadful, the field had been churned into mud by heavy rain, there was no shelter and many of the bedraggled prisoners were wearing their gas masks to keep the rain out of their faces. I tried not to sympathise and was rather pleased that they were guarded by black GIs who, it seemed to me, relished the role. I can imagine how the Nazis felt about it but would have liked some insight into the feelings of the black GIs. (On my first trip to the USA, some eleven years later, I got thrown out of the whites-only café in a Greyhound terminus because I tried to bring with me an Indian professor I befriended on the journey.)

Col. Winter had written to my father, a letter I did not read until I rummaged through my father's correspondence, after his death, over forty years later. There was a most curious aspect to it. Col. Winter kept stressing what a charming, good-looking and intelligent young man he found me to be, as though he feared that my father might otherwise reject me. It only occurred to me later that perhaps he had encountered cases where refugees remarried, fathered new families and did reject their offspring they had not expected to survive. In our close-knit family, the concept seemed so grotesque that it had never even crossed my mind, far less that of my father.

Around the end of April 1945, rumours began to circulate that Hitler was dead. I want here to return to the reason for my interest in the *Panzerfaust*. I had seen a poster instructing members of the Hitler Youth in its use. They were to have the honour of being the last line of defence. These young boys were ordered to crouch in a ditch holding the *Panzerfaust* on their shoulders until the enemy tank was almost on top of them. To do any serious damage, the tank had to be within about twenty metres. They might perhaps succeed in partially disabling it but, since killing all its crew was pretty well out of the question, it would have been a suicide mission. Hitler was here ordering the flower of the youth of his own beloved 'Volk' to lay down their lives at a time when it was absolutely clear that his deranged plans for subjugating the world lay in ruins.

These boys were to be the heirs and the future of his 'master race', not 'the others' – the Jews, Slav sub-humans, or the feeble-minded – but, in the end, when Hitler felt let down by his own people, when they proved unworthy of his insane schemes, he was ready to sacrifice them too. This, to my teenage mind, defined the demented evil of the man. At the time, I did not know that he died by his own hand in an underground bunker. Looking back upon it now, it seems just that the evil genius who cast a black shadow over all my childhood, who destroyed my wonderful family, among many millions of others, and who, but for the grace of God, so nearly destroyed me, ultimately perished like a rat in a sewer in the month of my seventeenth birthday.

I would like to think that there is an ultimate rightness – almost a natural law – ensuring that evil carries the seeds of its own destruction. Hitler was a hypnotic demagogue who had a genius enabling him to subvert a whole nation by working on its persecution complex. By persuading the Germans of the ludicrous concept that they were a master race, he managed to make them sub-human in their actions. But such evil incorporates a kind of stupidity, leading to fatal errors arising directly from its overweening misconceptions. Thus Hitler's arrogance caused him to take on the vastness of Russia, declare war on the USA (even while Roosevelt was still dithering) and repeatedly overrule his experienced generals. His fury over a token air raid on Berlin led him to order Goering to turn from destroying the RAF airfields to the revenge bombing of London, thereby losing the Battle of Britain and any chance of invading England.

Above all, the world was saved from Armageddon by his virulent anti-Semitism and insane rejection of 'Jewish physics' (a term which has about as much meaning as, say, 'Jewish rain').

It led to the exodus of the brilliant minds and outstanding experimentalists, the Albert Einsteins, Lise Meitners, Otto Frischs and others, and thereby ensured that the Manhattan Project was developed under saner sponsorship. Had Hitler been the first to acquire nuclear weapons, it would have resulted in a worldwide holocaust with deaths in the billions, not millions.

On 8 May, the war in Europe ended. Col. Winter drove me to Weimar in his jeep. There were no celebrations, needless to say, yet we had fireworks of a sort. German fighter pilots decided that being captured by the Americans was much preferable to falling into Russian hands. Many, making a dash from the Eastern front, tried to land near Weimar. Although the war had ended, the American pom-pom gunners clearly decided that while the planes were still airborne, they were fair game. The tracers made pretty patterns in the sky. I did not see any planes shot down, so perhaps they were just having a bit of fun.

PART III

The Return

10

Prague

When it became clear that there was no way for me to reach England without first returning to Czechoslovakia, I requested repatriation. The word 'return' here has a misleadingly cosy connotation of going back home, but I had no home to go back to. My father had arranged that I should lodge in Prague with a distant cousin of his, Hugo Lamač (Loewith, originally), of whom I had never heard before.

Those of us who wanted to go to Prague travelled in a requisitioned German wood-fuelled open truck. With the extreme shortage of petroleum, most non-military transport ran on the pyrolysis products of hardwood. Next to the driver's cab there was a large cylinder with a covered circular aperture at the bottom. Starting from cold required much patience and a flame. The driver, standing next to the vehicle, periodically tested the flammability of the gas emerging from the hole with his lighter. To begin with it was mostly steam. Eventually, depending on the state of the fuel, a roaring yellow flame stabilised, whereupon we all piled in and the driver diverted the gas to the engine.

The system had one great advantage: when we ran out of fuel, which happened before we covered much more than half of the 350-kilometre journey we were all sent to collect dry twigs in a nearby wood. That was just about adequate as fuel; had we depended on petrol, we would have been stuck.

We passed through Dresden, recently bombed into ruins, a desolate landscape of blackened rubble. Occasional walls left standing looked as if they might collapse on top of us at any moment. I must confess that pity for its former inhabitants was not my first reaction. I am still puzzled why some Germans hold 'Bomber' Harris responsible, rather than Hitler

'Uncle' Hugo strongly resembled my father in general build and stature During his former professional life he had been a judge in Slovakia. Among his souvenirs from that period was a Slovak goatherd's *kožáček*– a kind of walking stick with a small axe head instead of a handle – which was the murder weapon in a case over which he had presided. As he was married to a gentile, he had been deported only as far as Terezín, towards the end of the war – an unpleasant but generally survivable experience. They lived in a small flat near Staroměstské Náměstí (Old Town Square) with their daughter, Milenka, who was about three years my senior. They took me in and showed me great kindness, trying to feed me up in spite of their very limited postwar rations.

In Milenka's case, the great kindness extended to compensating for my years without any sight of the female anatomy. She arranged frequent displays of her body in various states of undress, which made a profound impression on me.

Handmade Buchenwald badge

The flat was a short walk from the offices which dealt with the flood of lost sheep like myself. I differed from the majority in knowing exactly where I wanted to go next – and as soon as possible.

I was given some cash and issued with a neatly tailored grey uniform with an artlessly handmade Buchenwald badge stitched on (another item now in the Imperial War Museum), which entitled me to free travel on all public transport and attracted much sympathy and goodwill. (It is only since I discovered quite recently that I ended up classified as a political prisoner that I have been wondering whether that might have had something to do with being treated as something of a national war hero.) Free travel enabled me to crisscross Prague on its many tram lines and revisit some of the sites I had loved as a child, and had dreamt about in the camps. Everything seemed somewhat smaller now than in my dreams (I must have grown) but it was all still there. By comparison with other European capitals, Prague had been left relatively unscathed. It struck me how much more durable buildings are than the loved souls associated with them. My one big excursion was by train to Ústí nad Orlicí.

I I

Ústí nad Orlicí

My visit lasted just a few hours, since I had to return the same day, having nowhere to stay overnight. A return train journey of over 160 kilometres plus the walk to and from the station did not leave much time at my destination, whatever that might turn out to be. I had only the vaguest intention of looking for people, places or possessions. Anything beyond seeing again the station from which we were deported, the town square and my uncle's house at 123 Rašín Street would be a bonus.

In the event, I found the only other survivor of the entire Jewish community: Mr Perlhaefter. Like Uncle Hugo, he had been deported much later and only as far as Terezín, thanks to being in a mixed marriage. He was a charming, erudite man, now much aged. He still sported the enamelled brooch – a replica of the yellow star – which he had sworn to wear for the rest of his life if he survived the war. He had also collected and kept the few treasured possessions which we had left with gentile friends in case any of us returned. There was my collection of minerals, including some semi-precious stones, the Voigtlander camera that had been my thirteenth birthday present and, above all, the treasured album of our family photographs. I left the stone collection, but the other links to the past are still in my possession today. Mr Perlhaefter died not long after my visit.

Of these remnants, the photo album was, and still is, my most cherished possession. The pictures begin with my birth and end with my first school days. It is difficult to explain the insecurity my experiences induced as regards my memories, but these photographs provide the only tangible testimony that my wonderful childhood actually happened and was not simply dreamed up during the nightmare of the camps. Here in these pages, frozen for all eternity, are pictures of the early years of mine and my little brother's lives, of our holidays in winter snow and summer meadows and of weekend trips on paddle steamers. They are in black and white and not of very good quality but they trigger my memories, invoking the details in sound and colour: the splash of the paddle wheels in the river, views of the sun-drenched meadows and vineyards alternating with crags with forbidding ancient castles brooding on top, and even my childish excitement when passing through the giant locks on the River Elbe.

In spite of all the indignities heaped upon us in Ústí nad Orlicí during the war, I came to love that little town and the beautiful forests and mountains surrounding it, so much that I revisited several times in later life. Before I finally write it out of this narrative, I want to relate some of the improbable coincidences that made those visits memorable.

I had to wait forty-four years to go back, because the Iron Curtain had descended. During that time my dreams of Ústí nad Orlicí acquired an almost mythical quality – partly perhaps because I could not safely go back during the Cold War and there was no one left in the world who shared my memories (in the meantime I had acquired a beautiful wife, three bright sons, British nationality, a Professorship at Imperial College, Fellowship of the Royal Society, some 150 publications to my name plus a couple of doctorates – so I could not exactly have spent all my time dreaming). However, in 1989, a pressing invitation to speak at a symposium in Prague persuaded me that, in spite of my loathing of police states, the time had come to take a calculated risk.

This was shortly before the Velvet Revolution. Rebellion was in the air and the streets were full of yellow security police cars. My wife and I were met at the airport by my host, the professor who organised the conference, and who had previously visited me in the UK. On the drive from the airport, I mentioned to him that I would appreciate the opportunity to visit Ústí nad Orlicí during some free time at the conference. I had thought in terms of being lent a car to drive myself, but it transpired that my status merited an official black limousine, a driver and a guide/interpreter (although I still retain my faultless Czech pronunciation, I have lost much of my vocabulary, which tends to land me in awkward situations).

It was to be another short but eventful visit. My uncle's house, having been requisitioned first by the German and then by the Communist administration, had been repainted externally so that I became unsure I had the right address. The house number was still 123 but the street had been renamed, Rašín having been replaced by a name from the Communist pantheon. Not one of the neighbours or passers-by could remember whether the street had ever been called Rašínova – or indeed had ever had a different name.

The Czechs have developed remarkable adaptations to being ruled throughout most of their history by one or other of their predatory neighbours; anyone who has read *The Good Soldier Schweik* will recognise the flavour. Once Big Brother decrees a change in the name of a street, by next morning total amnesia rules and no one remembers what the place used to be called. (I hope that does not sound derogatory; remembering all the innocent victims of Lidice, who would presume to prescribe heroism? Not I – having had to learn the lesson myself, as a good Czech, that bending is a much preferable alternative to being broken.) I would have left matters there, but my escort evidently felt that a gesture was called for and went to the Town Hall to interrogate the archives. The Town Hall was closed, owing to a lunch break which lasted until after 3 p.m., but thereafter we were most cordially received by the Mayor.

At this point, I must indulge in a flashback to the harsh war winter of 1941, when it was so cold that we skated in the streets on frozen snow, having had our skis confiscated by the Nazis, and when the Pick's domestic staff were forced to leave. Amongst them was the family of the housekeeper who lived in a flat in the house's basement. The housekeeper's son, Jaroslav was a mischievous nine-year-old. I remember him trying to persuade me to lick the door handle in bitterly cold weather and, although I would not give him the satisfaction of trying this while he was watching, having correctly suspected an ulterior motive, I was so curious to see what would happen that I tried it when no one was around. I had intended to try it ever so briefly but had clearly underestimated the thermal inertia and conductivity of a massive lump of brass, with the result that my tongue instantly froze to the metal and the resulting sore patch lasted many weeks.

The Mayor turned out to be a corpulent and pompous man, painfully conscious of his own importance. It seemed surprising that he would want to go out of his way to meet me and my little entourage. I worked out later that this was due to my interest in that particular address because, to my utter astonishment, the great man turned out to be none other but little Jaroslav who, half a century earlier, had introduced me to the pleasures of freezing my tongue to a door handle. Not that either of us recognised the other, although we had once lived under the same roof, but I warmed to him when it emerged that he recollected my uncle and the entire Pick family with genuine affection. He recounted some of the scrapes he got into with much glee and told me that Mrs Roubicek, the chauffeur's wife, was still alive. In return, I promised to send him copies of a photograph from the family album in which she appeared (see p. 40).

By now we were very late, especially in the eyes of the driver, who insisted on immediate departure and covered the return journey over very bad roads at amazing speed. I received no reply to my subsequent letter, which included copies of photographs I had promised to send, nor did I realistically expect any, since for a Communist mayor to have a pen pal in the UK would surely have caused some raised eyebrows in the Party.

My last visit, in 1993, well after the Velvet Revolution, was part of an extended holiday. The trip resonated with a wonderful feeling of liberation, the country being genuinely free again at last, and this time I resolved to remain for much longer. In Prague we stayed expensively at the Golden Goose right on Wenceslas Square and rented a Škoda for our travels. We visited Ústí nad Labem, now part of the most polluted area in Europe. The dead hand of the Communist regime had left its indelible marks everywhere. My childhood home now had a supermarket on the ground floor and the central square had been built over. We passed through Terezín on the way and spent some hours looking through the museum archives with archivists who were so helpful finding the records of all my family that I was tempted to offer myself as a stuffed exhibit in due course. The only surprise was the absence of any record of the Picks, which prompted the realisation that I had not seen my uncle's family on the day we were deported, or at any time since. It had never occurred to me that bribery might have been possible under the Nazis but perhaps if one had owned a factory . . . Hearsay had it that they perished in a labour camp in Kyjov.

In Ústí nad Orlicí we booked, for less than a tenth of the price of our Prague hotel, a large flat at the former government hostelry, which was being renovated, having been privatised in the somewhat optimistic anticipation of an influx of capitalist tourists. (The large numbers painted on the furniture and the way staff counted our towels and blankets before we were allowed to leave suggested they had not quite entered into the spirit of the new order.) Our room looked out onto the run-down premises of the school which I had so briefly graced with my attendance. As on previous occasions, my first walk was to my uncle's house. It was still number 123 but the street name had changed once again. This time I approved – the new name was Masaryk. Rašín had been Finance Minister in Masaryk's government and Thomas G. Masaryk, the President and founder of the first Republic, was the hero of my school days.

Under the Communist regime he had been written out of history, which struck me, during my previous visit, as being not only unbelievably petty but also a sign of deep underlying insecurity. Whilst I do not doubt that some of the Czech Communism was home-grown, I like to think that its mean-spiritedness was imported, as evidenced, for example, by the whitewashing of the memorial wall in Prague that carried the names of concentration camp victims during a period when the Kremlin flirted with anti-Zionist Arab states.

My uncle's house was in a state of disarray. It was being converted into a school for children with special needs and that also pleased me. The workmen allowed us in for one last look before knocking down partition walls. The wide wooden staircase which was being taken apart did not seem quite as grand to me as when I was a child but it was still fairly impressive. Now there would be no point in ever visiting the house again.

This time also I was able to retrace my old walks at leisure with my wife. The Orlice River in which we used to bathe with my mother was heavily polluted but the forests, the footpaths and the mushrooms were still there. Walking to the hut at the peak in search of bread with real butter would now have been beyond either necessity or my physical endurance, but we drove all the way to the top, along much-improved roads, and had lunch there alongside locals with their bags bulging with boletus and other edible fungi. It remained a wonderful unspoilt place and that evening we had a dinner party there with Jaroslav, his wife and a very ancient gentleman whom I had never met before but who turned out to have been an accountant in my uncle's factory – he must have been in his late eighties. Jaroslav was no longer Mayor, which he appeared to find rather more surprising than any of us did. However, he seemed less bitter than resigned to yet another strange turn the world had taken. He behaved as if a great weight had been lifted from his shoulders and, on this occasion, chatted much more freely about old times, and drank an alarming number of toasts to the memory of former friends and acquaintances.

On our last morning we visited the cemetery where my legs, remembering no doubt the many pilgrimages with my aunt and the two Waldis, astonished me by carrying me automatically to the Pick's family vault without any help from my brain. Alice Pick's name is, of course, the last one engraved on the stone, but nearby there is a small memorial to all the Jewish families who died in German concentration camps. I imagine that must have been due to Mr Perlhaefter, whose grave is also nearby. All the Jewish graves were beautifully kept. With Mr Perlhaefter's death, the former Jewish community of Ústí had died out. (We, the Weinbergs, did not count, having only ever been birds of passage.) So the Germans succeeded in divesting this small town of its Jews but the Czechs still remembered them and tended their memorials in the graveyard.

PART IV

England

12

A Lancaster Bomber

In spite of the kindness of uncle Hugo and his family, I was desperate to join my father in England as soon as possible. Not only was Czechoslovakia haunted by too many beloved shadows whom I needed to banish from my thoughts if I was ever to have a future, but now there were ominous signs that an Iron Curtain might descend and perpetuate the separation of the only two remaining members of our family.

Unbeknown to me, sometime during the summer of 1945, the UK government agreed to admit 1,000 orphans under the age of sixteen who had been freed from the Nazi concentration camps. It was probably just as well I did not know, because I failed to meet the criteria. I was not an orphan and was over seventeen, and it would have never occurred to me that I might be able to hitch a lift. So the invitation to present myself at an address in Prague for an immediate flight to England came as a wonderful surprise. I learned much later that fewer than 750 children could be found who had survived the camps so there were many vacancies. The planes taking us to the UK were

RAF bombers. They became available after bringing Czech pilots, who flew with the RAF during the war, back home to Prague.

Uncle Hugo gave me a small battered cardboard suitcase and an ancient Omega watch (still in my possession) as a parting gift. Apart from my photo album and the few treasures from Ústí, there was not much to pack. The address to which I had to report turned out to be a Prague recuperation home, which was already full of children who had been brought there from Terezín. I had to spend a night there due to delay caused by some kind of hitch with the planes.

Eventually, however we were bussed to Ruzyne Airport where we climbed into stripped-out Lancaster bombers. There must have been about ten of them and I could barely contain my excitement. We sat on the floor. I got a place under the plastic astrodome in the middle of the plane but could only see a fragment of the sky above.

On the way we landed in Holland for refuelling. Some kind local ladies had set out refreshments and goodies for us on trestle tables, so they must have been forewarned of our arrival. I walked around the plane, inspecting the outside, and remember being vastly impressed by the size of the undercarriage. The wheels and tyres towered above me. Recollecting my last close encounter with a plane – the Sabena Junkers Trimotor in 1938 on our return from Belgium – brought home to me the massive growth in aircraft size that had been brought about by the war.

We landed at RAF Crosby-on-Eden, somewhere near Carlisle, and so I was in England at last – after an eventful postponement of almost seven years. My first act of celebration was to haul myself up into the bomber's observation dome, breaking the glass on my uncle's Omega watch in the process.

I do not remember much of our reception beyond kind faces, more goodies, some formalities and much hanging about. There were only about half a dozen Czech boys – and two girls – each with a parent or close relative in England, among perhaps three hundred, mostly Polish, orphaned children, who had no reunion to look forward to. We were all to be transported to a camp near Windermere, as soon as formalities were complete. That journey, however, I do remember vividly.

Unlike the smaller children, who were taken off by bus, we older boys had to climb into the back of a tarpaulin-covered truck. The back was just a hinged panel with the space above it open to the chilly intermittent drizzle. Nobody had warned me about English summer weather. I must here also admit to having taken up smoking after liberation, probably as a result of GIs generously handing out precious cigarettes, which had previously been regarded as valuable currency. Moreover, in the interest of my 'waste not, want not' instinct, I had acquired a cigarette holder in the form of a disgusting little pipe which enabled me to smoke butt ends, including those which my friends might otherwise have discarded. The journey of some sixty miles took us over undulating roads which seemed more like a fairground rollercoaster, more so even than the bumpy flight in the Lancasters. I do not normally suffer from travel sickness. What pushed me over the edge, I think, was fizzy ginger beer – a beverage completely new to me. Our driver stopped at a pub and, being a kindly man, wanted to treat us. The ginger beer was the outcome of our ignorance of English pub fare and lack of communication. All I can say is that it is not to be recommended in conjunction with smoking fag ends and lurching about in the back of a truck.

The histories of the Polish orphans have been written up in Martin Gilbert's *The Boys*. Sir Martin was unaware of our small group of Czech boys – unsurprisingly, since we disappeared from Windermere within a few days of our arrival.

I must confess that, at the time, I could not warm towards the Polish boys. I have been strictly honest in this narrative and I must be honest about this also. Some of the older lads took so much food that there was not enough left for the rest; they also helped themselves to the villagers' bicycles and acted as if such behaviour were a clever joke of which they might be proud. We, of course, thought it an inexcusable abuse of English hospitality, especially as the locals were so trusting as not to lock their bikes. (It may well be that I have been unduly sensitised by Nazi propaganda and racial stereotyping of some kind of behaviour which made it so abhorrent to me that, to this day, I can not see it as a harmless practical joke.) That does not detract from the enormous admiration I have for how those children subsequently made their way in the world, without the support of relatives.

Just arrived in England, in my Czech uniform.

I am convinced that there must be an error on the third page of my Alien Registration Certificate, which says: 'Permitted to land at Crosby-on-Eden on 17th August, 1945'. That date was handwritten by a police officer at Preston police station, at a much later date. I am sure that I arrived in England on 14 August, because the next day was V-J day, 15 August 1945. The reason I am so certain is that I was quite unable to contact my father by phone or telegraph, since nothing and nobody worked. Officially, a two-day holiday had been declared and in the euphoria which marked the final end of World War II, none of the switchboards was (wo)manned on that day.

13

My Father

As camps go, Windermere was more in the holiday camp than the concentration camp category. I believe that it had been built for aircraft factory workers during the war. Over the V-J holiday, before our fathers came to collect us, we had a good time. We must have been given some petty cash because my friends and I were able to hire rowing boats on Lake Windermere – great fun, in spite of the recurring drizzle.

My father who, at that time, worked as a chemist at the Manchester Oil Refinery and lodged as a 'paying guest' in Worsley, a suburb of Manchester, turned up in a Bentley; regrettably not his. The magnificent vehicle was driven and owned by a most imposing middle-aged lady whose position must have matched her appearance since, in addition to the Bentley, she evidently had enough petrol for the return journey from Manchester to Windermere, which in those days spoke volumes about her standing, importance or wealth. She was a friend of another Czech boy's father, a Manchester doctor, who had also come to collect his son. There were three of us Czech boys who all had relatives in the Manchester area and who remained good friends ever since.* We all had different camp histories but had not known each other before meeting in Windermere.

I find it difficult to describe the anticipation and emotional upheaval of seeing my father again. I remember being deeply shocked by his appearance. He looked like an owl to me because of the dark circles under his eyes. In some ways I felt very close to him – somewhere within this stranger was the darling daddy of my childhood, the hero soldier of whom I had been so proud. But the nearly seven years of separation had made the moat between us deeper than could be rationalised. Looking back now, I realize that the big change was in me, not in him. He was, after all, only forty-seven years old, an age when seven years normally do not bring about great change. I, on the other hand, was no longer a child and had been completely transformed in those lost years by going through more tribulations than most people experience in their lifetime.

There is one thought I must dispel at the outset. I suspect that some members of my family thought that my father should not have 'abandoned' us, or perhaps should have ridden to our rescue on his white charger once it had become clear we could not get out. The lack of understanding by the postwar generations of how things were then seems odd to me but it should not come as a surprise. If a thousand people get killed in attempting

---

* They are all mentioned in the acknowledgements. Otto and I overlapped in Auschwitz but he knew me only as the boy who ladled out the soup. Peter was the boy who lost his toes but we did not meet before the flight to England.

a heroic act, the one who happens to survive by blind chance, records his story, which is then remembered and thus distorts history. That may be what I have been doing in these pages, though I have tried not to. It never crossed my mind, nor my father's, that his journey to England was anything other than the necessary first step in trying to get us out of Czechoslovakia. He could not even join the Allied forces because of the importance to the war effort of his oil sulphonation research work at Manchester Oil Refinery.

I can imagine how much he suffered once the first reports of Nazi atrocities began to leak out. My father was never any good at expressing emotion, or too good at suppressing it. I had never seen him weep and thought that he was not capable of it. All he ever said to me that gave any clue to his internal turmoil was that he sometimes became aware of his aberrant demeanour from the way fellow commuters stared at him.

The chronicle of my experiences only came out in dribs and drabs over the next few years. One of the first questions my father asked was: 'I suppose there is no chance . . .' He let the question regarding the survival of his wife, child, father and sister hang in the air – and I just shook my head. Just on the basis of sheer improbability it would have been wrong to raise his hopes. It was never mentioned again. That created a massive taboo area, a block of memories which we tiptoed around. We never looked back.

Another topic that never came up for discussion, to the best of my recollection, was that we might return to Czechoslovakia.

In retrospect I find that surprising because I know it was seriously considered by some of the other 'Czech boys'. But we had nothing and nobody to return to now, only distressing memories. Besides, my father had become an Anglophile. One of the first things he said to me was, 'You will be surprised by the decency of the man in the street.' I soon came to understand. All men may be born equal but there is much to be said for achieving democracy through evolution rather than revolution (since 1642, anyway), for not having been invaded since 1066, for having a largely ceremonial Royal Family and no secret police. It seems to have conferred upon the English a certain generosity of spirit and easy self-assurance.

My father's first preoccupation was to fill me up with nourishing food. Since this was during the days of rationing in the immediate aftermath of the war, he decided that we needed to live on a farm. While he was arranging that, I shared his lodgings in Worsley, but soon thereafter we moved to an ancient farmstead mass-producing turkeys in the middle of nowhere. It was reached from the main road by half a mile of narrow hedged lane across acres of pastures providing grazing for a few horses and a large heard of cows. Clearly there would be no shortage of milk, eggs and meat.

The dwelling, however, proved something of a culture shock. My bedroom, in the coldest corner of the building, had some features which were totally new to me, such as a tiny fireplace, a copper bed-warming pan, a stoneware hot-water bottle, a sideboard with a chinaware basin and a water-jug which froze over in the following cold winter. The fireplace was clearly so totally ineffective that there would have been no point lighting a fire.

There was also something vaguely disturbing about the farming folk. The patriarch seemed too old and arthritic for any hard work. His son, who must have been in his twenties, had suffered an accident with a pitchfork at some time, which had left him with a deformed skull. During our time there he shot a rat in his parents' marital bed. Although he used only an air gun for this purpose, we became alarmed when we saw blood-soaked bed sheets being carried out, wondering if someone had been murdered. Whatever was wrong with his sister seemed to require industrial quantities of Dettol, judging by the aroma following her use of the bathroom, which we shared with all the family.

The long lane leading to the farm was unlit and pitch-dark at night. When I returned after sunset, I had to carry a small torch for cowpat avoidance. The horses in the adjacent field had a perverse sense of humour combined with an ability to move about stealthily in absolute silence. When they sensed me coming, they stretched their muzzles invisibly over the hedge and snorted loudly just above my head, making me jump out of my skin. Perhaps the sight of people with their hair standing on end gave them a bit of a giggle.

The farm, however, fulfilled its main purpose. I had egg and bacon, or gammon with apple sauce, for breakfast every day. (I never got used to eating gammon with apple sauce and separating one from the other to create a second course tended to make me late in the mornings, but that was a minor quibble.)

At the weekends my father and I went on all-day hikes, exploring the glories of the Peak District. In this respect we reverted to the holiday routines of my childhood, except that I was no longer the tired little boy trailing behind. We shared a love of nature – which he inculcated in me when I was a small boy. As he aged, he became more enamoured of big trees as living memorials to the past. I could not call him a tree hugger because trees of small enough girth to embrace were not nearly as interesting to him as some giant old oak of which he could say, 'Look at this tree – it has been here since before the discovery of America.' We talked all day about everything but the past. It was a new relationship. We had become friends. Close good friends.

14

Natural Philosophy

And so, halfway through my eighteenth year, having all but forgotten how to write (see my signature on p. 149) since the ignominious end to my schooling at the age of twelve, I started on my secondary education in a language in which 'not in front of the children' was about the only phrase I could remember. At the same time my father asked me what kind of career I wanted to pursue, and I decided that I would like to be a journalist. The thought of being sent to exotic locations to report on exciting events appealed to me. Curiously, it never occurred to me that there might be a language problem.

My father said, rather cunningly, that anything would be acceptable to him, so long as I took a degree first. The first objective then was to obtain the Northern Universities Joint Examination Board School Certificate, which would admit me to university by the end of the academic year. That could clearly not be achieved through the normal school system, even if an educational anomaly such as I could have gained admittance.

The particular back door through which my father squeezed me was a wretched commercial college catering chiefly for shorthand tuition but also had crammer classes for previous School Certificate failures. With one or two exceptions (other flotsam and jetsam of the havoc wrought by the war years) my fellow students were not the brightest stars in the scholastic firmament, but the teachers loved my maturity and eagerness. I came to realise just how exotic I must have seemed when one of my new friends – a Lancashire lad some two years younger than I – commented on how difficult it must have been for me to learn to eat with a knife and fork!

One consequence of my alien allure was that I received frequent invitations to weekend parties from one or another of my many female classmates. My father must have become alarmed because he reacted by unobtrusively leaving a condom for me on the mantelpiece, with the murmured advice that he was 'not yet ready to become a grandfather'. That, incidentally, was the only piece of paternal sex education I received in my entire life. My father rightly surmised that I would be quite incapable of buying such a thing myself but completely wrong in conjecturing my need for it. At that time, thanks to my restricted social contacts during the war years, I was very shy, socially inept and tended to spontaneous blushing. It was several months before I ceased to regard girls as creatures from another dimension altogether.

I should like to be able to say that I worked hard; that would be something one might be proud of. But it would not be true. I had been deprived of learning for so many years that I soaked up any interesting information like parched soil soaks up its first rain shower. I was doing what I most wanted to do, and not for the sake of passing exams but to start filling a bottomless well of curiosity that had been frustrated for too many years. I developed a heretical hypothesis that my lack of schooling may, bizarrely, have proved to be an advantage because I never got put off learning. Here is the proof: although I missed half of first term and had the additional burden of having to learn English, I passed, after only sixteen weeks of actual tuition, the School Certificate with distinctions in all the science subjects, in English literature, in pure and applied mathematics and, unsurprisingly, in German. I got credits in the rest, including English.

I ought perhaps to comment here on the pitfalls of regarding Shakespeare's plays as tutorial material for Foreigners learning English: only sensitivity to listeners' reactions will indicate, for example, that 'gadzooks' has passed its sell-by-date as an exclamation or that 'scurvy knaves' has, somewhat illogically, evolved into 'bastards'. The most surprising exception to my examination successes was a bare pass in Czech, in which I was fluent. This was an act of revenge, according to my father, by the Czech examiner, who hated the thought of having to return home imminently.

On this evidence, I do not think that we do our children any favours by forcing them into education at too early an age. There is a risk that at least some of them will be put off school and learning. We all start with an innate human curiosity and thirst for knowledge but I believe that can be stifled if we make children feel coerced. Once we make them feel that education, involving hours of tedious homework, is an imperative to further their careers – in which we have a vested interest – the joy of learning may be lost forever.

If it is true that nobody forgets an inspirational teacher, it must be because they are in short supply. I encountered only one inspirational teacher in my undergraduate life. It came about through an oversight of my father's, or else his quite unreasonable faith in my abilities. I believe that he wanted me to study chemistry. He was motivated, I suspect, partly by the wish that I should follow in his footsteps and partly by his ambition for me to marry, in due course, the daughter of the Chairman of ICI or some other baron of the chemical industry. What follows is the story of how I failed on both these counts and became a physicist. Chemistry in the 1950s, particularly organic chemistry, leant heavily on having a good memory and, in view of the patches of amnesia during periods that I did not care to dig up from my subconscious, I started with a huge preference for understanding rather than memorizing.

My father's slip-up was that he entered me for both Mathematics and Applied Mathematics – one subject more than was required to pass the Northern Universities Joint Examination Board's School Certificate (my two foreign languages added another to the surplus). When it transpired that the wretched commercial college that I attended did not have anyone capable of teaching applied mathematics, my father enrolled me for additional evening classes at what was then Bolton Technical College. There I fell under the spell of a young mathematics teacher who actually understood and loved his subject. He had a pocket full of needle-sharp pencils and could draw perfect circles freehand. Mathematics, mechanics, hydrostatics, properties of matter, as explained by him, all made such perfect and obvious sense that there was never a need to remember anything.

I had not come across algebra or even negative numbers but before long I started playing around. I remember one instance when I became intrigued by the question of how many roads could be constructed between an arbitrary number of towns. Having deduced the equation, I was surprised to note that the number of roads remained positive for some negative numbers of cities; moreover you could have one road joining minus one city. To his undying credit, my tutor did not laugh when I asked him what that could possibly mean – he was actually taking my games seriously!

All this led to a turning point in my life. Here was a world of infinite calm and depth, totally separate from the turmoil of human emotions, in which one could unearth profound truths about nature from simple experiments and mathematics. This world offered a boundless vista of cosmic riddles – a world of logic and beauty, where human emotions and suffering were, thankfully, totally irrelevant. One could, perhaps, even earn a modest living trying to solve the crossword puzzles set by the ultimate authority – almost a religious activity. I had found the path to salvation from the mayhem of my childhood.

I could not gain immediate access to university with my non-existent educational background. In addition, I believe that the government had also imposed a compulsory quota of ex-service personnel on universities after the war. Fortunately London University had an enlightened policy of External Degrees at the time and courses at lesser institutions could be registered with the University for these degrees. I registered as an External student at South West Essex Technical College in Walthamstow, first for a General B.Sc. and a B.Sc. Special Physics a year later. After my first year, and a grilling by their Education Committee in Chelmsford, I was awarded a major maintenance grant by Essex County Council.

At the same time, my father had parted company with the Manchester Oil refinery, over some patent rights I believe, and became Chief Chemist of a newly formed company in Harlow. Here he set up a new laboratory in an industrial park with the aim of generating new products in food chemistry and adhesives. When time permitted, I was free to play around in the brand-new lab. The owner of the company bought Rowney-bury House in nearby Sawbridgeworth and gave my father a bungalow, which must have been the gatekeeper's cottage, for the two of us to live in.

All this took a very long time to arrange and, in the meantime my father and I moved a great deal, from one guest house to another in the Woodford and Wanstead area. I had to commute to college every weekday but that opened up the glories of Epping Forest for our weekend walks. These tended to last all day. We took off in the morning with sandwiches and walked until sundown, re-establishing a treasured childhood ritual.

He never tired of hearing about my new insights into physics, and I spent many hours trying to share with him such exciting perceptions as, for example, how with a few pieces of glass and using simple interferometry, one could measure distances with the resolution of the unimaginably tiny wavelength of light, or the dazzling leaps of imagination involved in relativity and quantum theory – running entirely counter to everyday experience – illuminating the fundamental absolutes of our universe. He always listened with genuine interest and some regret at having missed them himself in his youth. In what other field of human endeavour has there been such an enormous explosion of knowledge within one generation?

There were some unexpected social advantages to South West Essex Technical College. Amongst the student body, scientists were in a minority. Our Special Physics class consisted of seven students (of whom two passed – and we were considered to be a specially promising year). I met a wonderful girl who was studying English, French and Geography, with whom I shared almost sixty years of my life, and three loveable sons, until she died, two years after our Golden Wedding anniversary.

After I met her, there were fewer weekend and more after-dinner walks with my father. He liked Jill well enough – it was impossible not to, I believe. In his eyes she had only one major shortcoming; she was definitely not the daughter of the Chairman of ICI, and as I spent more and more time with her, he worried I might miss out on that opportunity altogether. So I did not become a chemist (though I took chemistry as far as my

General B.Sc.) and did not marry into the upper echelons of the chemical industry.

It took me a long while to realise, with some astonishment, that only a small subset of people see the world as I do; that most others are content to use phones, watches, radios, computers without the slightest need to know how they work. I have no proselytising zeal in this respect. In fact, when I became an academic, I always refused to offer positive advice to students who, after graduation, came to ask me whether they should stay on to do research. I told them that it meant having little money, deferring having a family, and if they needed to ask, they probably ought not follow that path.

I came from a home filled with music and poetry. For many years I continued to write poems for my father on his birthday. I continue to love the arts but only for my own entertainment and as a spectator. There is a genuine difference here between the arts and sciences. In science, it is not necessary to be a genius to add some small but useful piece to cumulative knowledge and share in the glory of understanding its entirety – hence the truism about standing on the shoulders of giants and seeing further than they. I discovered that this is not just a cliché when I was revising for my physics exams. Since I could not rely on remembering mathematical derivations of physical theory, which were a major feature of our exams, I always closed my books and tried to deduce them from first principles. This had three possible outcomes. Most often I got stuck – after which the elegance of the approach by the appropriate 'giant' came as an indelible revelation. Sometimes I had the satisfaction of getting there on my own. Very occasionally, I came up with an alternative derivation – a special kind of triumph for an undergraduate. All these outcomes, however, were deeply satisfying and unforgettable (which was the purpose of the exercise).

So I became a physicist. The main reason was the overwhelming majesty of the revelations in the subject that made all else look trivial by comparison. Even if one might not be able to work at every cutting edge, one was equipped to follow and understand. What poem could compare with the poetry of understanding that we are actually made from the debris of stars – truly children of the universe? What other subject is logic, philosophy, poetry and religion rolled into one? To borrow the words of Kip Thorn, 'the amazing power of the human mind – by fits and starts, by blind alleys and leaps of insight – to unravel the complexities of our Universe, and reveal the ultimate simplicity, the elegance and the glorious beauty of the fundamental laws that govern it.'

My father died in the ninetieth year of his life. He had been present at the Royal Society ceremonies associated both with my election to the Fellowship and, later, the award of the Rumford Medal, and I believe these and other similar occasions helped him to become reconciled to my having taken up physics rather than chemistry. In his later years we lived on opposite sides of Richmond Park and I was able to cycle to see him at the weekends. We walked in the park, which is full of ancient oaks. I was fortunate to have had my father around for so much of my life.

Appendix

Chronology 1942–1945

25 December 1942	Pardubice to Terezín
15 December 1943	Terezín to Auschwitz-Birkenau
7–8 July 1944	Selected for slave labour camp and sent to Blechhammer.
	The last time I saw my mother and brother.
10–12 July 1944	Auschwitz-Birkenau *Familienlager* liquidated
1 January 1945	Russian offensive starts. German forces retreat.
	Decision to liquidate Silesian camps.
21 January 1945	Start of the 'death march'* from Blechhammer
2 February 1945	Reached Gross-Rosen concentration camp

---

* Probably now called a 'death march' because some 800 of us who could not keep up were shot and thrown onto horse-drawn farm carts which brought up the rear. We, the few who survived the war and the majority who perished in the camps, did not use and would not have understood terms such as 'Holocaust' or 'death march'. These were coined later, by outsiders.

7 February 1945	Boarded open carriages on train to Buchenwald
10 February 1945	Arrived Buchenwald; few left alive
11 April 1945	Buchenwald liberated

Felix Weinberg died on 5 December 2012, at the age of eighty-four. Emeritus Professor of Combustion Physics and Distinguished Research Fellow at Imperial College, London, he was still working and planning the final revisions to this book as well as conference papers for the future. He was the author or editor of four books and more than 220 scientific papers. Internationally acknowledged as a leading thinker in his field, he was awarded a D.Sc. by the University of London (1961), both the Silver (1972) and the Bernard Lewis Gold (1980) Medals of the Combustion Institute, Fellowship of the Royal Society (1983), the Royal Society's Rumford Medal (1988), the D.Sc. Honoris Causa by Technion, Haifa (1990), the Italgas Prize for Energy Sciences (Turin Academy, 1991), and the Smolenski Medal of the Polish Academy of Science (1999), as well as being elected to the American National Academy of Engineering as a Foreign Associate in 2001. The Hugh Edwards Lifetime Achievement Award for contributions to Combustion Physics was conferred on him in 2005 (Institute of Physics).